AF594726

Cincinnati Characters

Cincinnati Characters

The Unknown, Unappreciated, and Unhinged

Written by Brent Coleman

Illustrated by C.F. Payne

Orange *frazer* Press

Wilmington, Ohio

ISBN 978-1949248-494

Published for the copyright holder by:
Orange Frazer Press
37½ West Main St.
P.O. Box 214
Wilmington, OH 45177

For price and shipping information, call: 937.382.3196
Or visit: www.orangefrazer.com

Illustrations: C.F. Payne

Cover and book design:
Orange Frazer Press with Catie South

Library of Congress Control Number: 2022904622

First Printing

Acknowledgments

I am thankful for my wonderful wife Lauren, our kids Alex and Will, my close friends and the colleagues I learned with and from. Also, thanks to editor Dave Caudill, to the *Enquirer* and WCPO as well as my only journalism instructors: Liz Lillard (junior high), Pat Presto (senior high) and Art Nauman (college).

—*Brent Coleman*

Contents

Introduction

I was in my mid-twenties reporting at a small California newspaper when my mother launched what I call "B.J.'s Clipping Service." For more than thirty years, she sent me articles from my hometown. Many featured people she thought I knew or were about Palo Alto's historical houses being replaced by McMansions. Also about this time, she revealed that she had been her Iowa college's newspaper editor during World War II. I was amazed and proud to put to use the journalism and history genes I inherited.

That first job led to thirty-five years in "newspapering" that started with reporting, shifted to editing and ended with writing again. History, which I minored in at college, and houses were my key subjects late in my career in historically rich Cincinnati. I moved there from Sacramento at age thirty, anxious about the abrupt change but confident I could handle it. After all, both my parents were Depression-era Midwesterners.

This book's breezy profiles are versions of articles I wrote for all ages after my twenty-six years at the *Cincinnati Enquirer*. I did them at the same time I wrote weekly, in-depth pieces on more than 200 Greater Cincinnati homes, many of them historical. I dove deep into who had lived in these houses and made people central to many stories. The WCPO.com history column they spawned was a natural. Overall, I published more than fifty stories about mostly-forgotten, nineteenth century folks and those known by name only.

I met C.F. Payne after reporting on the rehabilitation of an 1800s downtown home in which Chris painted a whimsical mural. We became friends, and I'm thrilled to work with such a renowned illustrator. We hope you find what we've created is fascinating and entertaining. Go ahead, read it any way you want to—from front to back or by jumping around.

Cincinnati Characters

Rees Price

Eccentric developer spread city west

Rees Evan Price, the only Cincinnatian whose name graces three neighborhoods, was the kind of character adults might want to meet over a pint of beer. Oops. You better make that a water. That's about all Price drank.

The early nineteenth century developer of what is now called the Price Hill Incline District was so devoutly dry that he didn't drink tea or coffee. Cincinnatians of his time called his estate "Buttermilk Mountain." It was said that the sour milk was the strongest drink you could find at the many picnics and gatherings held on the estate grounds that Price (1795–1877) dubbed "Mount Zion."

Everyone knew Price's clean-living rules. Tavern owners on West Eighth Street—on which horse-drawn wagons called "Price's Chariots" transported goods from downtown Cincinnati—had a little fun with the pillar of their community by naming their establishments First Choice, Next Chance and Last Chance, which was closest to the base of alcohol-free "Price's Hill."

Price's eccentricities exceeded his love of water. He had legendary strength and was a strict Protestant and anti-Catholic, who dressed like a simple farmer and ate only vegetables and fruit, except for apples, of course, because they are forbidden. He was a Christian who drummed to his own beat, favoring the right of women to vote and staunchly opposing slavery. Price and his wife believed they could connect with the dead, hosting many seances with their older children and friends in their home.

Price wrote unusual—Cincinnati history blogger Greg Hand called them "delightfully loony"—theological essays, hand-delivered them to newspaper editors for publication and asked that they share with him any criticism his ideas inspired. He was known to sign the letters "Rees Price, Prince of Peace." Some editors called him "The Prophet."

Price went beyond using the power of his pen, according to Hand. "He was well known as a street preacher in Cincinnati, known as 'Father Price,' and was often found declaiming to the crowds along the riverfront wharves from atop a pile of salt barrels."

"(Price) believes the Bible but interprets it by the spirit within him," wrote Methodist Episcopal Church Bishop and Western Christian Advocate editor Thomas Morris in an 1819 article. "Upon the whole," Morris continued, "he is the most pleasantly deranged man with whom I am acquainted."

Politics stirred Price's soul as well. Angered by the federal government's intent to annex Texas in the mid 1840s, he climbed a large eagle in the U.S. Senate chambers and shouted his opposition in the name of Almighty God, newspapers reported. The Senate adjourned without voting on the matter. Some reports said authorities briefly jailed Price after his outburst.

Price was a native of Wales who came to Baltimore with his family as a little boy. When Rees was in his early teens, his family floated by flatboat to Cincinnati when its population was just 2,500. The handsome, strong and intelligent immigrant laid bricks and farmed as a young man. He went on to make a fortune building where his father's development efforts had failed—above a bare Ohio River and Mill Creek ridge where the land was wild and the air cleaner than in the smoky, industrial valley. The new community became the gateway to Cincinnati's vast western hills.

In 1824 at age twenty-nine, Price married up in class to prominent judge John Matson's twenty-one-year-old daughter Sarah. But he refused to accept his father-in-law's wedding gift of eighty-two-acres far west of downtown in Home City (today's Sayler Park). Eventually, Price owned the land, but not until he had earned enough money to pay for it. The hard-working Price founded a sawmill and a brickyard and developed what became known as Price's Hill.

The Price estate sat on a square block anchored at the corner of Mount Hope Avenue and West Eighth Street, now home to the Incline Theater. The

Prices hosted many celebrations and outdoor performances in their estate's heyday. But as the years passed and Price became more reclusive, it was more of a quiet and spiritual haven.

Rees and his wife, whom he called Sallie because his mother and sister were both Sarahs, had eight children. Sons William and John partnered to build a 350-foot-high incline railway, construction starting in 1872 and ending in 1879, two years after Rees died. Unlike other Cincinnati inclines, Price Hill's featured a track for people and a track for freight. Another son, Rees B., was a beekeeper and part owner of a dairy in Home City.

Today, the most prominent artifact of Rees Price's little kingdom is a brick home that was William's on the southeast corner of Hope and West Eighth. In addition, there is Price Avenue and Rees E. Price Academy, a public elementary school located a mile away. The Price land, developed in what was then called Storrs Township, is now East Price Hill and is flanked by two of Cincinnati's other fifty-one neighborhoods, Lower Price Hill and West Price Hill.

Price was called "General" for the rank he had held in the Ohio State Militia. The "general" became so wealthy through development projects that he was able to finance his sons' Price Hill Inclined Plane Co. It operated for sixty-eight years and opened up western Hamilton County for farmers who helped feed the city's nearly 300,000 residents.

General Rees E. Price was worth more than $6.5 million in today's currency when he died in 1877 at eighty-one, succumbing to "congestion of the lungs." His family's Spring Grove Cemetery plot—located a short walk from grand monuments of early jurist Jacob Burnet, American wine industry founder Nicholas Longworth, mattress makers George Stearns and Seth Foster and pioneering merchant Joseph Carew—is marked by a modest stone that belies a man of his stature.

Founding Fathers

Ohio River settlements trace to six pioneers

Six men established three settlements within several months in Hamilton County in 1788. They qualify as Cincinnati's Founding Fathers, left to right in illustration: John Cleves Symmes, John Filson, Matthias Denman, Robert Patterson and Israel Ludlow and Benjamin Stites (not shown).

All jockeyed for the land, but the winners of the river trade competition were Denman, Patterson and Ludlow, who settled 800 acres of a fertile basin Filson helped them find. It became Cincinnati.

These Founding Fathers' stories are deeply intertwined. They shared eastern roots, war experience and the Ohio River. They shared the goals of clearing land and providing food, shelter and security. And they shared fear, death and flight from Indians defending sacred hunting grounds.

John Cleves Symmes (1742–1814)

Territorial Judge Symmes was more taker than giver. Thanks to his role as a Continental Congress delegate, he became the first major land owner in the Northwest Territory at age forty-six in 1788, spending $82,198 (about $3 million today) for 250,000 government acres called the Miami Purchase, which was bordered by the Ohio, Great and Little Miami rivers and an undocumented northern line. He was known to sell the same land to two different buyers and other parcels that he didn't even own. His sporadic record keeping and resulting lawsuits doused Symmes' dreams. He fell into debt and died penniless at seventy-one. His name, however, lives on in the community names Cleves and Symmes Township. Symmes' daughter, Anna, married future president William Henry Harrison, whose son, John Scott, was the father of president Benjamin

Harrison. That makes John Cleves Symmes the only American to have a son-in-law and great-grandson to be president. His nephew, John Cleves Symmes Jr., was well known as an advocate of the pseudoscientific Hollow Earth theory.

Captain Benjamin Stites (1746–1804)

Early Limestone (Marysville), Kentucky, trader Stites, forty-two, marveled at the Ohio River Valley's beauty and potential as he was floating down the Ohio on fifty-by-sixteen-foot flatboats with about twenty-six brave men and women, mostly from New Jersey. His November 1788 settlement, called Columbia, featured a granary and soon included fifty cabins, a school, church and graveyard. The last of Columbia's cabins washed away in 1815 and the villagers moved to higher ground. The former Pennsylvania tax collector's life soon became complicated by marital strife. He had two illegitimate wives who bore him six children. He died at fifty-eight and is buried in Pioneer Cemetery, the only remaining artifact of Columbia. It's on a hill near Lunken Airport.

Matthias Denman (1760–1838)

Denman was a speculator and the financial whiz among the founders. The New Jersey native made and sold buckskin britches, dabbled in agriculture and horsemanship and was a minuteman and private in the Revolutionary War. From his outpost in Limestone, he traveled the region buying forested land as far west as Louisville. At thirty-seven, Denman paid $500 (about $10,000 in today's currency and twice seller Symmes' purchase price) for the Cincinnati basin. Denman made Filson and Patterson—later Ludlow—equal partners and became Cincinnati's main recruiter of settlers. He made his money selling off his third of the basin and left little mark upon his departure in 1804. He returned on horseback numerous times and died at age ninety.

Robert Patterson (1753–1827)

Ohioans associate his name with Wright-Patterson Air Force Base near Dayton. Robert was the first Patterson to impact the region. The second was his grandson, National Cash Register founder John H. Patterson. Colonel Patterson helped found Lexington and Georgetown, Kentucky, in the 1770s. The

Pennsylvania native became familiar with the western frontier while fighting in the Revolutionary War alongside Daniel Boone and under George Rogers Clark. After settling Cincinnati and fighting Indians, Patterson moved his family to Dayton in 1802 and built a grand estate in 1816 named Rubicon. He died at seventy-four and is buried at Woodland Cemetery adjacent to his land.

John Filson (1747–1788)

More than two months before his partners, Denman and Patterson, and his replacement, Ludlow, set up at Cincinnati's Yeatman's Cove in December 1788, Filson vanished. The forty-one-year-old Pennsylvania teacher, soldier, surveyor and the first biographer of Boone disappeared into the first-growth forest west of Cincinnati. His body was never found, and Indians were blamed. Filson had begun to plat the new town and intended it to be called Losantiville, the "L" being for the Licking River that merges with the Ohio at Cincinnati; "os" for mouth in Latin; "anti" for across from (the Licking) in Greek; and "ville," French for town. Northwest Territory governor General Arthur St. Clair often is credited with changing the name to Cincinnati in 1790, but other accounts, such as those written in 1844 by the settlement's legal authority, Judge Jacob Burnet, credit the name to Ludlow. It honors the Revolutionary War officers' club called The Society of Cincinnati, and was used before the settlers arrived in 1789.

Israel Ludlow (1765–1804)

The twenty-three-year-old New Jersey native platted a north-south grid for Cincinnati and Hamilton, thirty miles north. He platted Dayton, as well, and drew the north-south line for the seminal Greenville Treaty of 1795 that forced Native Americans to leave Ohio. Ludlow was one of the first settlers to venture north of Cincinnati. In 1790, he established Ludlow Station on 125-acres in today's Northside neighborhood. It became a haven for adventurous pioneers but proved to be unsafe and closed in 1794. Ludlow was back two years later, building a mansion with orchards and beautiful gardens on a nearby Mill Creek bluff. He and his wife, Charlotte Chambers, entertained many dignitaries, including Miami chief Little Turtle. Ludlow died in 1804 at thirty-nine. A Northern Kentucky town is named for his son, Israel L. Ludlow.

Little Turtle

Miami tribe war chief turned peacemaker

When Ohioans and Hoosiers think of the great Indian chiefs that ruled their region more than 200 years ago, it is likely the names Tecumseh and Blue Jacket come to mind. After all, both Shawnee leaders have been depicted stereotypically on American television and in Hollywood movies for decades.

Perhaps the name Little Turtle wasn't strong enough for scriptwriters, but the war chief of the Miami tribe for about thirty years left a legacy equal to those of his more famous counterparts, not just for his conquests in battle, but for his peacemaking with the territorial and federal governments.

The six-foot-tall Little Turtle was at first an enemy of the U.S. government. But once he signed the Treaty of Greenville in 1795, he never raised another weapon in battle.

He sat at the tables of some of the region's most powerful men, such as Cincinnati founding father and city surveyor Israel Ludlow and future president William Henry Harrison. He met with George Washington in 1797, and posed for the great American portrait artist Gilbert Stuart. In the following years, Little Turtle convened with presidents John Adams and Thomas Jefferson.

His impact on Cincinnati and the region during the two decades after its 1788 founding is represented by a bronze statue of the Miami chief above the south bank of the Ohio River where it absorbs the Licking River in Covington, Kentucky.

Little Turtle was "remarkable for his mental vigor and great common sense as well as for his skill as a military leader," wrote Charles T. Greve in *Centennial History of Cincinnati and Representative Citizens.* The Miami chief's Indian name was Mishikinakwa. He was born twenty miles north of Fort Wayne, Indiana, in 1752 to Miami chief The Turtle and his Mohican wife. Little Turtle rose to power following the Miami nation's victory in battle against a French ally of the Americans in 1780.

Little Turtle earned fame when he led Miami, Shawnee and Delaware Indians to victory in battles against U.S. troops led by General Josiah Harmar and General Arthur St. Clair, both based at Fort Washington in Cincinnati. In the 1791 battle known as St. Clair's Defeat, the Indians killed more than 600 soldiers in what several sources say is the worst defeat ever suffered by the U.S. Army in its decades of fighting Native Americans.

Little Turtle's Indiana village was destroyed by General James Wilkinson's expedition in that year, but it did not vanquish the Miami. Little Turtle, whose daughter had been captured during a Kentucky militia raid, led attacks on army supply lines in 1794. His intent was to keep General "Mad" Anthony Wayne from establishing outposts from which he planned to grab more western Ohio and eastern Indiana land from the Miami.

Wayne, who also commanded from Fort Washington, gathered a force of 2,000 and marched northward in August 1794 in hopes of ending the Northwest Indian War. They encountered the Miami, led by Little Turtle, and the Shawnee, led by Blue Jacket, at Fallen Timbers near modern day Toledo, Ohio. Wayne won in resounding fashion.

The Indians' loss at Fallen Timbers taught Little Turtle that the Americans had superior numbers and weaponry. Greve quoted the chief as saying: "We have beaten the enemy twice; we cannot expect always to do this. The Americans are now led by a chief (Wayne) who never sleeps. The day and the night are alike to him. I advise peace."

Little Turtle represented eleven tribes and helped negotiate the Treaty of Greenville in 1795. He was one of the last to sign it and vowed he would be the last to break it.

The Miami retreated to the Fort Wayne, Indiana, area, having given up 25,000 acres of their land to the United States by signing the treaty. The once-mighty military leader then turned his efforts to breaking his people's dependence on alcohol and shifting their economy to an agricultural one with help from Quaker missionaries and the federal government. A teaching farm established for the Miami, however, failed after a few years.

Little Turtle traveled to the East Coast several times and brushed shoulders with Washington in Philadelphia. In his dealings with the white world—during which he would dress half as an Indian and half as a white man—he "became quite intimate" with French intellectual Count Constantin-Francois Chasseboeuf and accepted two handsome pistols from Revolutionary War hero Tadeusz Kosciuszko of Poland, according to Greve.

Little Turtle signed four treaties from 1803 to 1809, actions that lost him the respect of many in the Miami nation—and his leadership role. Little Turtle died at age sixty, reportedly of gout.

A plaque at his burial site in Fort Wayne honors him for being "Teacher of His People. Friend of the United States." His influence in Indiana and Ohio was widespread, reaching as far as Westerville, Ohio, in the ironic form of the Golf Club at Little Turtle.

In his 1904 book, Greve shared a one hundred-year-old story about Little Turtle's visit to Ludlow Station, Israel Ludlow's roadhouse north of Cincinnati. Historian Edward Deering Mansfield was at the station to visit his father, surveyor Jared Mansfield, who was drawing lines for the Treaty of Greenville. Little Turtle was staying at Ludlow Station as well, and the younger Mansfield wrote the following about his encounter with the peace-making chief:

He had wit, humor and intelligence....As he rode away from the house in the declining sun, I might without any violent stretch of imagination have seemed to see the last great spirit of the Indian race leaving the land of his fathers looking for the last time upon the beautiful valleys of the Miamis and bidding farewell to each hill and wood and stream forever.

IV

Martin Baum

Taft Museum of Art lives in his home

You know that old building in downtown Cincinnati that looks like the White House and is home of the Taft Museum of Art? You might know some names in its ownership lineage: millionaire wine maker Nicholas Longworth, millionaire pig iron industrialist David Sinton, newspaper editor Charles Phelps Taft and his philanthropic wife Anna Sinton Taft.

Many have heard of those folks. But an important name is missing from that list, the name of the man who had the place built in 1820. Let's put Martin Baum on your radar with the Longworths, Sintons and Tafts, because, just as they were, he was a key player in the development of Cincinnati.

Baum arrived in Cincinnati in about 1795 (a decade before Longworth), seven years after the town was founded. Fewer than 500 people lived in its ninety-four log cabins and ten framed houses. Baum's first home was right on the river.

What Germany native Baum did in Cincinnati's rough-and-tumble early years was brave and ultimately phenomenal. He opened a general store and formed an export company that morphed into the first bank in the West. Baum founded the city's first sugar refinery and steam mill, ran iron, cotton, wool and whiskey businesses and spearheaded the creation of the first public library, the Literary Club of Cincinnati and the Western Museum. He served one term as mayor, was asked but refused to serve in Congress and was a pillar of the Presbyterian Church, the town's first house of worship.

Baum became the richest man in Cincinnati, a man who needed a house fit for entertaining the town's who's-who and visiting dignitaries, as well as his fellow Germans who turned to him for hope and opportunity.

Gorham A. Worth—cashier of the local chapter of the United States Bank of which Baum was the first president and whose Mount Auburn house may have inspired the design of Baum's—had this to say in his 1851 memoir, *Recollections of Cincinnati*: "He was a man of great probity of character, of plain manners and sound sense and ranked for many years among the first and wealthiest merchants of the place."

Martin Baum was born in Germany in 1765 and came to America with his family as a boy, settling in Hagerstown, Maryland. According to historian George Katzenberger, Baum's parents sent their son to school in Baltimore, where he studied German, French and English as well as some Latin and Greek.

Baum wanted to become a physician, but he must have felt an overwhelming curiosity for the West, because he joined the Army instead, serving under General "Mad" Anthony Wayne to fight Native Americans in Ohio. Baum was put in charge of medical supplies and ran the apothecary at Greenville Fort. He was there for the final fight, which was the Battle of Fallen Timbers, on August 20, 1794.

Baum came to Cincinnati at age thirty. It's possible that he traveled with a surveying team led by John Cleves Symmes, who owned much of the land in Southwest Ohio. That trip broadened Baum's sense of opportunity.

Katzenberger said Baum possessed "great initiative" and "decided talent for business," which he applied to his two-story general store near the Ohio River. His success earned him a spot in Cincinnati's small circle of leaders, which included fellow German and the city's first mayor David Ziegler, as well as Judge Jacob Burnet. In 1804, Baum married Burnet's sister-in-law, Ann Somerville, in the judge's house.

The Baums built a brick house next to their general store and had seven children from 1804 to 1820, the year he built his now famous white house. Those between years saw Baum grow his many businesses and speculate on land from Cincinnati to Yellow Springs and Toledo.

Land speculation in the West was rampant in the second decade of the nineteenth century, and it got Baum and the nation into big trouble. Debts couldn't be paid, businesses buckled and banks foreclosed on many homeowners. Ultimately, the U.S. Bank's western branches, Cincinnati's included, pulled the plug on the capital train, catapulting the economy into its first great financial panic in 1819.

"The city at large groaned under the infliction for many years," Worth wrote. "Mr. Baum, however, I have understood, still left at his death a very considerable estate."

The foundation of Baum's wealth may have been his house and his friends, one of whom was his neighbor, wealthy land surveyor William Lytle II. Businesses bottomed out during the three-year depression, and Baum's certainly took a big hit, enough so that in order to pay off his debts he offered to sell Lytle his Pike Street house and the nine acres around it for $62,000.

In a letter, Baum, who had ten or more relatives living in the house he called Belmont, wrote to Lytle that "I must have $1,000 or thereabouts in advance because without some money I and my family must starve."

Lytle liked the deal but insisted Baum throw in seven additional land lots to increase its value to $155,000 (more than $2.6 million in today's currency). Baum balked and deeded the house and half his acreage to the U.S. Bank for $50,000. The bank leased the estate to a "school for young ladies," according to a 1998 article by Jayne Merkel for the Cincinnati Historical Society. Nicholas Longworth purchased Belmont for $28,000 in 1830.

Baum bounced back from his financial low. Among his accomplishments in the final years of his life was the establishment of cotton trade with the city of Liverpool, England. Baum died during an outbreak of influenza in 1831, the same year Lytle II died of tuberculosis.

Baum's family buried him at the Presbyterian cemetery where Washington Park is today. His remains were moved in 1853 to Spring Grove Cemetery, where his befittingly tall monument can be found in Section 97, Lot 10.

FINDLAY MARKET

James Findlay

General marked more than market

Findlay. It's the name of a Cincinnati street and one of the country's oldest public markets in one of the city's oldest neighborhoods, Over-the-Rhine. But when ten Cincinnatians were asked who Findlay was, the one answer other than "no" was actually a question: "Wasn't he a Civil War general?" No. James Findlay died twenty-six years before the war began and seventeen years before the establishment of the public market that bears his name.

Yes, he was a general...and a state representative...and the mayor of Cincinnati...and a four-term congressman...and an unsuccessful candidate for governor of Ohio. But doesn't it seem odd that few people know this and the many other contributions Findlay made to the early development of the Queen City?

Findlay was born in Pennsylvania in 1770, came to Cincinnati five years after its 1788 founding, became an attorney, established the city's first general merchandise store in a log cabin on the banks of the Ohio River, and entered politics as Cincinnati's third mayor (1805–1806). In addition, he was a brigadier general in the Ohio Militia and a colonel in the Second Ohio Volunteer Infantry during the War of 1812.

Findlay, who was a Democrat before there were Republicans, served as an early member of the Territorial Legislature and held several federal positions, United States Receiver of Public Monies and U.S. Marshal among them. He invested in the Cincinnati Bell, Brass and Iron Foundry along with Cincinnati legends General William Henry Harrison and Judge Jacob Burnet. Findlay helped found the U.S. Branch Bank with the same two men and a dozen others, and he was instrumental in the establishment of Cincinnati's public library.

Still, he is best known for the public market, which he envisioned being a place where businesses could sell their wares and woodsmen and farmers from outside the city could sell their goods and fresh crops.

Findlay was born into a family destined to achieve. He and his oldest brother attended public schools, and John went on to serve in the Pennsylvania House of Representatives. Another older brother, William, had an even more impressive career. He served as governor of Pennsylvania, in the U.S. House and Senate and was director of the U.S. Mint. Both men outlived their little brother James.

Findlay lived in Cincinnati during an era of steady growth—in agriculture, commerce, manufacturing and banking—despite there being a fury of fires, floods, epidemics and other catastrophes. He witnessed wars and treaties with Ohio River Valley Indians and was attacked and nearly killed near Portsmouth, Ohio, while transporting cargo during the pre-steamboat era.

During the War of 1812, Colonel Findlay led a regiment near Detroit and supervised construction of a fort near what is now Findlay, Ohio. The British captured and imprisoned Findlay at one point.

After the war, he continued to invest in Cincinnati land as well as businesses. A large tract of forest he owned just north of downtown between the base of Mount Auburn and what is now Liberty Street was known as "Findlay's Woods." He and partner Jepthah Garrard platted the unincorporated Northern Liberties neighborhood (Over-the-Rhine today)—named so because it was free of city regulations and taxes—in 1833, and named streets such as Race, Elm, Green and Findlay.

The partners also established an open space on Elder Street for a public market, but Findlay died of a "cold" at age sixty-five before any market buildings could be built. His dream wasn't realized until 1852, following the 1851 death of his wife, Jane "Jenny" Irwin Findlay. His descendants made the market happen. The Findlays were re-buried in 1854 in Spring Grove Cemetery. Its records do not indicate the couple had children.

What kind of man was Findlay? The answer to this question was difficult to find. Historical websites supplied the basic facts of his life, but not of his personality.

One source held promise: The 1856 memoirs of Gorham A. Worth, who lived in Cincinnati from 1817 to 1825 and was cashier of the U.S. Bank, which Findlay helped establish, and owner of what is thought to be the oldest home (1819) remaining in Mount Auburn. Worth's memoir, *Recollections of Cincinnati*, was reprinted in 1916 by the Historical and Philosophical Society of Ohio and is online in its complete form. The following excerpt about James Findlay was lifted from Worth's chapter titled, "Prominent Citizens of Cincinnati:"

General Findlay was the last of a race of men now utterly extinct. A race that formed the connecting link between the old school and the new, between the cocked hats and powdered pig-tails of the revolution, and the plain, straight-haired democracy of Mr. [Thomas] Jefferson's day. Still, in honesty and patriotism, as well as in air and manner, he leaned, I think, more to the former than to the latter. An honester man in deed never lived. He was frank, open, warm-hearted and hospitable.

...There was no subject upon which he did not entertain certain notions, and notions too, that were exclusively his own. He had been a general of militia, nay, he had, like other patriotic gentlemen of the west, volunteered his services and entered the army in the campaign of 1812, under the heroic [General William] Hull. He had, of course, seen some service, though [thanks to his commander-in-chief] not much fighting. The campaign, however, gave him the right to dispute with General Harrison upon military etiquette, military history and military law.

Findlay trivia is plentiful:

- His family did not pronounce the "d" in their name. Some relatives went so far as to change the spelling of it to "Finley."
- General Harrison and his wife Anna Symmes Harrison had ten children. The only one who did not live into adulthood was James Findlay Harrison, whose name was a nod to the close friendship the great men shared.
- Cincinnati had nine public markets at one time, of which Findlay Market is the sole survivor. It was placed on the National Register of Historic Places in 1972.

Eliza Potter

Hairdresser's book shook high society

Eliza Potter's celebrity was a flash in the pan. Yet during a two-year period leading up to President Abraham Lincoln's first term, she was the talk of Cincinnati—and all because of a little book the free and Black hairdresser wrote when she wasn't combing the hair of the city's wealthy white brides, belles and beautiful ladies.

Potter's book was juicy and gossipy at a time when tell-alls were few and far between—and when few Black women wrote, let alone published books. Titled *A Hairdresser's Experience in High Life*, it rocked the town. "Hairdresser" quickly became a best-seller among whites wondering who were the subjects of Potter's sharp, witty descriptions of small-talk secrets and social posturing.

Eliza C. Potter, known as "Iangy," was an independent and free, light-skinned Black woman living an Ohio River crossing away from where slavery was the norm. Strife over slavery was bubbling, which meant that gleaning gossip about women living the "high life" was risky business for Potter and required stealth. Writing and publishing a book about it took great courage.

Potter's book was among the first to include criticism of slaveholders, the nouveau riche, and undignified and immoral people of high standing. Potter, however, was much more than a groundbreaker. She was a homeowner and a single mother of two stepchildren whose father gave them their last name but apparently little else.

Potter first traveled as a maid with wealthy families to Europe, where she witnessed the baptisms of the Prince of Wales and the Count of Paris as well as the funeral of the Duke of Orleans. Potter also "dressed and combed" the rich at trendy retreats in New Orleans, Saratoga, New York, and Newport, Rhode Island.

Even more impressive for a young "mulatto" woman—as she was described in the 1860 Census—Potter spent three months in a Louisville jail before defeating charges that she broke the law by telling a Kentucky slave how to escape to Canada.

Potter is remembered, albeit by few outside a niche of historians, as the writer of a unique and poignant book. The thirty-something hairdresser brushed over very little, wielding a "bold if not polished pen," noted Nikolas Huot in *American Authors, 1745–1945*. And although she was described by another historian as being "reckless and sometimes rash," Potter showed some caution. She used code names for the women and families she wrote about. She referred, for example, to "Miss J," "Mrs. W" or "Miss FF."

Potter didn't even put her name on her book, although it was well known she was its author. She kept her background secret, too. She said she came from New York, but she didn't name her parents or mention her maiden name.

Where Potter was born isn't certain. History detectives found records from later in her life that indicate she was born in Virginia and once lived north of New York. Perhaps caution motivated Potter to claim northern roots while she was living near slave states. Such a claim would make her safer from slave hunters.

Genealogical tools and historians have since filled in blanks in Potter's story, but no photograph of her has been found. She came West to chart a better life course and chose Cincinnati, likely because it had the largest African-American community in the Northwest Territory.

There were opportunities to work as a maid or a wet nurse in the Queen City, where she settled in the Little Africa neighborhood near the Ohio River. Potter also joined St. Paul's Episcopal Church and began to work her way into the homes of wealthy whites. Somehow, she became stepmother to two children named Potter, indicating she married a second time.

Potter "combed" as many as fifty women a day while on retreats abroad, and her work in Cincinnati was successful and well-known—as was Potter the person. The 1860 U.S. Census shows she lived with her stepchildren, Kate and James, and a young apprentice hairdresser named Louisa Taylor near the city's shopping and cultural center. Her neighbors were a mix of Blacks and whites, mostly working-class people with families.

Potter worked for whites as if invisible. Being of mixed race—as was the case with successful photographer James Presley Ball and renowned landscape painter Robert Scott Duncanson, both of whom likely knew Potter—gave her "the ability to cross racial and social boundaries" and become part of "the Black nouveau riche," wrote one historian.

Potter's home, according to the 1860 Census, was valued at $2,000, and her personal property amounted to $400—more than $65,000 combined in modern currency. Yet for unknown reasons, the Census showed her living in Niagara, New York, seventeen days after the Cincinnati recording. Had the secrets Potter shared in her book the year before played a role in her seemingly sudden departure? Most likely. She had ruffled many feathers and lost many clients.

Her death remained a mystery for decades until genealogist Reginald Pitts discovered her death notice in Rye, a small town in West Chester County, New York. The date on the notice was 1893, which would have made Potter seventy-three, possibly a little bit older since her birth date documents have not been found, which is normal for a Virginia-born slave.

Ilustrating how Eliza Potter was a "stranger in a strange land" is a memory made in England that she included in "Hairdresser:" "My little charge wanted me to call him Master, but I told him I would not do so, if he were as old as Methuselah. I will leave that word for the South, where it is exacted."

The book in its original state was reprinted in 1991 by Oxford Press and is for sale online. A more accessible version published in 2009 includes an introduction, insightful annotations and historical updates by Black American studies scholar Xiomara Santamarina. It is available in hardcover, softcover and Kindle versions.

Charlie Gould

'Bushel Basket' only native on first Reds team

Charles Harvey Gould was a man of firsts. He was the first first baseman of the first professional baseball team in America, the 1869 Cincinnati Red Stockings. He was the first native Cincinnatian to play pro ball, and he was the first manager of the second edition of the Red Stockings, which became today's Cincinnati Reds.

The fans, called "cranks" in that era, knew Gould as "Bushel Basket," at six feet the tallest man on the team. His large hands—though smaller than an eighteen-inch-wide bushel basket—rarely "muffed" a ball.

Various accounts of the end of the Red Stockings' record eighty-one-game (some sources say eighty-four, even ninety-seven) winning streak on June 14, 1870, blame an errant throw by Gould for allowing the Brooklyn Atlantics to win in the eleventh inning. And his record as player-manager of the 1876–1877 Red Stockings—an almost completely new team in the brand new National League—was a dismal 11–77. The team pulled Gould from his management role halfway through its second season, after which he resigned.

Off the field, Gould was somewhat of a wanderer, according to a 1984 article by University of Cincinnati archivist Kevin Grace in the journal of the Society for American Baseball Research. Charlie married Ohioan Laura Netherly in about 1874 and had five children, one of whom died in infancy. But he never settled on a career, starting as a secretary and groundskeeper for the Red Stockings and then bouncing around from job to job: police court officer, deputy sheriff, streetcar conductor, railway clerk, bookkeeper and insurance agent.

Census records from 1860 to 1910 listed Gould as living at a different Cincinnati address every ten years. His wanderings ultimately ended at the home of his son in Flushing, New York, where he died at age sixty-nine in 1917. Gould was buried without a marker in his family's plot at Cincinnati's Spring Grove Cemetery. Today, however, a large headstone honoring Gould that was installed by the Reds in 1951 stands in Section 67, Lot 54.

Gould, one of eight children of George Gould and Elizabeth Fisk Gould, was born August 21, 1846. His father was a successful produce merchant on Cincinnati's waterfront. Charlie helped keep the business' books and began playing organized baseball at fifteen.

Legend has it that at one point in his youth, Gould won a contest by throwing a ball one hundred yards. But it was catching one without a glove that became his expertise. Throwing to him was as easy as throwing to a bushel basket, his teammates said.

The Cincinnati Base Ball Club brought in English cricket star Harry Wright in 1868 to be team captain. Wright assembled the best players possible—Gould included—to compete in the amateur National Association of Base Ball Players. The team went 41–7, but team president Aaron Champion and Wright wanted to do better. So they pooled club members' money and exploited baseball's 1869 lifting of its no-pay rule.

Wright received a $1,200 salary. Gould pocketed $800. The other players, all of whom except Indiana native Calvin McVey came from East Coast teams, split the remaining $10,000 payroll.

The Red Stockings' strategy worked. They went 57–0, and cranks swarmed games as the team barnstormed cities from New York to San Francisco. The ten men traveled by carriage, train and boat from April 17 to November 5. They sported hand-sewn, white flannel uniforms with knickers, long red stockings and a big red "C" on their chests. The previously aloof press loved them.

Cincinnati was in a fervor over their Red Stockings as the team racked up one win after another against both professional, amateur and hybrid teams, according to Harry B. Ellard's 1907 book, *Base Ball in Cincinnati: A History.* Local boy Gould was a fan-favorite.

“He was one of the best-humored men on the ball field, always working with a will, and always to be found at his post...As a first baseman he was one of the best, and, considering the swiftly thrown balls he had to handle, he nevertheless got them all,” wrote Ellard.

The city welcomed the Red Stockings home on July 1, 1869, overjoyed by their unparalleled success, which included a 16–5 win against the Washington Nationals that was attended by President Ulysses Grant.

“When the [team’s] train rolled into the Little Miami depot...about half of the town’s population was there to welcome the conquering heroes. There was a parade from the depot to uptown. Houses along the route were profusely decorated. The popular idols took all the adulation in stride,” reported a Cincinnati newspaper. The following day, Gould, his mates and Champion were presented with a wooden bat that measured twenty-seven feet long and nine and a half inches thick at the handle.

Charlie Gould received a $50 bonus. But because a gambling and drinking culture and financial debt cursed the Red Stockings, the team split up at the end of the 1870 season. Wright started a professional team in Boston and chose his brother George, Gould and McVey to move with him. Wright described the players left behind as “drinkers, growlers and shrinkers.” The Cincinnati Red Stockings, with new owners and mostly new players, would not swing their bats again until 1876.

Gould helped the Boston Red Stockings to one championship in two years in the National Association of Baseball Clubs before leaving to play for lesser teams. He played first base and managed the new Cincinnati Red Stockings in 1876–1877 before retiring at age thirty. For a short time thereafter, his team duties included buying balls, never again catching or hitting them.

Gould left the team around 1879, taking with him a career batting average of about .260 along with buckets of memories and a glowing reputation. Archivist Grace wrote that “Gould wasn’t a great manager, and although he was a superb fielder, he was only a fair hitter. But he was a baseball pioneer, a witness to new eras in this city’s history and his country’s pastime.”

Ben and J.S. Harrison

Little-known leaders fathered two presidents

Relatively speaking, after the presidents Adams and before the presidents Bush, there were the presidents Harrison: the ninth elected leader of the United States, William Henry Harrison (bottom left in illustration) and his grandson, the twenty-third president, Benjamin Harrison (bottom right).

William Henry, a Native American fighter, frontiersman, slave owner and founder of North Bend, Ohio, was best known for being elected president under the campaign slogan, "Tippecanoe and Tyler Too"—and dying after just one month in office.

William Henry's grandson, a quiet man known affectionately as "Little Ben," was a Cincinnati native, Miami University graduate, lawyer and statesman whose legacy lives on in his hometown of Indianapolis but is mostly unappreciated elsewhere.

William Henry's and Benjamin's stories are well-documented in countless history books and websites. The stories of their respective fathers—Benjamin Harrison V and John Scott Harrison—rarely are told. Here they are:

Benjamin V (1726–1791)

Benjamin Harrison V (top left) was a Virginia plantation and slave owner. Accounts say the big man had an equally large personality that intrigued some of his fellow Founding Fathers, including George Washington, but irritated others, John Adams among them.

In line to sign the Declaration of Independence, "Big Ben" Harrison (1726–1791) reportedly said to the man standing next to him, the future vice president under James Madison, Elbridge Gerry:

I shall have a great advantage over you, Mr. Gerry, when we are all hung for what we are now doing. From the size and weight of my body I shall die in a few minutes and be with the angels, but from the lightness of your body you will dance in the air an hour or two before you are dead.

Benjamin V's family came from England to Virginia in the 1630s. His father and two of his nine siblings were killed by a lightning strike when Benjamin V was nineteen. The tragedy influenced his choice to discontinue his education at the College of William and Mary in Williamsburg.

Benjamin V inherited the bulk of his father's estate and headed up the family's Berkeley Plantation for the rest of his life. Harrison's wife was Englishwoman Elizabeth Bassett. They had seven children, William Henry (1773–1841) being the youngest. Benjamin V sent William Henry to college to study medicine but died before witnessing any of his son's many adventures and accomplishments.

At age thirty-two, Benjamin V was elected to the Virginia House of Burgesses, where he served split terms. He was among the first to protest English taxation of imported goods by King George III. That same year, Benjamin V was one of seven Virginians selected to serve in the first Continental Congress.

He shared a house with George Washington while living in Philadelphia during the second Continental Congress in 1775 and signed the Declaration of Independence there in 1776 but left Congress in 1777, serving Virginia as its governor from 1781 to 1784. A staunch opponent of centralized government, he refused to sign the Constitution in 1788 because it lacked a Bill of Rights.

Benjamin Harrison V died in his home following a dinner party in 1791 and was buried at Berkeley Plantation, the beloved home he rebuilt after it was ransacked and partially burned by turncoat Benedict Arnold in 1781.

John Scott (1804–1878)

One might think being the only American whose father and son served as president would be what history buffs remember most about two-term Cincinnati Congressman John Scott Harrison (top right). That would be true if it weren't for a little body snatching incident in late May 1878.

John Scott (1804–1878) was born to William Henry and Anna Symmes Harrison in Vincennes, Indiana. He studied medicine and served on the Cincinnati College board of trustees at age twenty, but later switched to farming his father's North Bend land. John Scott's first wife, Lucretia Johnson, bore him three children but died at age twenty-five. He married Elizabeth Irwin a year later, and she birthed ten children. The Whig Party called on John Scott to run for Congress, and he won a seat in 1852. He switched to the Opposition Party in 1853 and was re-elected, but he lost his campaign for a third term in 1856.

He sold the Harrison family estate in 1871, keeping just six acres, which included the family home of his father-in-law, land baron John Cleves Symmes, and the presidential tomb of his father. When John Scott died at age seventy-three in 1878, he was considered to be a very old man and wore a fashionably long gray beard. He was buried in one of the twenty-four vaults in the Harrison Tomb—but not for long.

Within a day of his death, John Scott's body was snatched. His son, John, was unaware of the theft. But while coordinating a search for the stolen body of a family friend, he shockingly found John Scott's desecrated body dangling from a rope in a downtown medical school shaft. It was put there for students. Newspapers around the country referred to the macabre incident as "The Harrison Horror."

People criticized the lack of security at the Harrison Tomb. Some suggested its inhabitants be moved to Spring Grove Cemetery. That didn't happen. But three years after the body snatching, Ohio legalized the sale of unclaimed bodies for scientific use, in effect, eliminating the demand for stolen corpses.

Thirty years later in 1910, the spectacular body snatching story still resounded with American newspaper readers. A little-known Cincinnati crime reporter and later a famous music critic named Henry E. Krehbiel, who had been working across the street from the medical college on that awful day, gave *The New York Times* this quote he got from a tearful Benjamin Harrison:

And out of the hole in the floor hanging by his neck, a hook under his ear, stark naked, with his gray beard and his hair shaved off, for he had already been on the table, came my father!

William Dickson

Judge advised Lincoln, led Black Brigade

Most visitors to Smale Riverfront Park in downtown Cincinnati fail to stop at the bronze statue of William Martin Dickson. His name is not easily recognizable, and that's too bad. A closer look shows his stamp is all over the nation's nineteenth century history.

Dickson was a judge and an abolitionist, who headed an all-Black unit that fortified Cincinnati against a looming Confederate Army invasion in September 1862. At first, police seized free Black men and directed them into a mule pen. But when Dickson got the job to lead them, he changed things.

Dickson sent the 400 detained men home for the night, and asked them to report in the morning. Those 400, plus 300 more, showed up. He named the non-military workers the Black Brigade of Cincinnati and let them design and fly their own flag. He gave his men fair wages for their fifteen days of service. In appreciation of Dickson's fair treatment, the brigade presented him with an engraved sword in a ceremony that the Smale Park statue re-enacts.

Dickson had an impact on national events, as well. Specifically, he shared a strong bond with President Abraham Lincoln, to whom he will be forever connected by family and the violent ways in which they died. Dickson and Lincoln married blue blood Kentuckians and first cousins Annie Parker and Mary Todd, respectively. The men became personal and political friends in the newly formed Republican Party. A serious intellect, Dickson wrote Lincoln a persuasive outline for freeing the slaves that likely encouraged the president's issuance of the Emancipation Proclamation.

Americans know about our sixteenth president. Few, however, remember Dickson: the son of a poor Indiana preacher; the self-supported Miami

University student; the Harvard University Law School graduate; the successful lawyer and judge; the week long tour guide of the future president; the organizer of the Black Brigade; the stealthy politician; the author-advocate; and the most notable victim of the worst public incline accident in the city's history.

Dickson's father, Jacob, was an Indiana minister with two sons, John and William. William was born "weak" in 1827, so John had to work a trade to help the family make ends meet after their dad died in 1837. William's role was to get an education, which took more strength than he was thought to have.

Dickson walked miles to school in Madison, Indiana, toting books and enough food for each week he was away from home. He took night classes at Hanover College, worked as a janitor and got into Miami University, graduating fifth in the class of 1846 at age nineteen. Dickson then worked as a teacher and studied law on his own. He earned a Harvard Law School degree, passed the bar in Lexington and met his future wife there in 1850.

Dickson didn't think he could afford to court Annie Parker. Regardless, he bought five tickets to an upcoming concert by Swedish songstress Jenny Lind. He sold two to cover his costs and invited Parker and her father to attend the show. They obliged, and the ensuing courtship culminated in marriage in 1852. Soon, Dickson joined the law firm of Alphonso Taft, patriarch of Cincinnati's famous political family, which included his son, President William Howard Taft.

In September 1855, Dickson and his wife hosted Lincoln, who had been hired to assist a team of defense lawyers in a federal patent case being tried in Cincinnati. The Dicksons offered the country lawyer the Southern hospitality he appreciated, so he stayed in their downtown home.

The legal team, which included Lincoln's future Secretary of War Edwin Stanton, would not let the gangly Lincoln to be in court. Stanton went so far as to call Lincoln a "long-armed ape." He was "humiliated and mortified," Dickson wrote for *Harper's Weekly* years later.

Lincoln, who was paid $500 in advance, used his free time to see the sights. For about a week, Dickson acted as Lincoln's guide. They visited

Belmont, the downtown mansion of winemaking millionaire Nicholas Longworth that is now the Taft Museum of Art. They toured Spring Grove Cemetery and called on the nearby home of manufacturer and art collector Jacob Hoffner.

Still, the future president was unable to hide the disappointment of being banished from court. "He attached to the innocent city the displeasure that filled his bosom," Dickson wrote. Lincoln reportedly said: "I have nothing against the city, but things have happened here as to make it undesirable for me ever to return." (He came back twice.)

Dickson's star rose in step with Lincoln's, particularly as an abolitionist. He traveled to Washington in his advisory role to Lincoln, Stanton and Salmon P. Chase, who, as Ohio's governor, had made the thirty-two-year-old Dickson a common pleas court judge in 1859. He later shared a successful downtown law practice with two of his sons.

A debilitating illness in 1866 lingered for the rest of Dickson's life but did not stop his progressive pen. He published dozens of articles and pamphlets in the last twenty-five years of his life, attacking "monopolies, jobbery and public trickery, public dishonesty and office seeking for the mere office," according to S.B. Nelson's 1894 book, *History of Cincinnati and Hamilton County, Ohio.*

An operating engineer took the blame for the October 1889 Mount Auburn Incline crash that killed Dickson. Crew members had oiled the twenty-one-year-old, 2,000-foot-long incline earlier that day. But the easy fix failed. Historian John H. White, Jr. wrote about the ensuing crash: "The impact sounded like an exploding boiler—the air was filled with flying bits of glass, wood, and dust. The car body wrenched loose from the truck frame and hurled itself into a grocery store across the street; the roof of the car sailed down Main Street a full one hundred feet."

Dickson died along with five others and was buried at Spring Grove Cemetery, thirty-four years after visiting there with his cousin, Abraham Lincoln.

Clara Baur

She made a city a classical music mecca

That she called herself the "directress" speaks volumes. Clara Baur appeared petit, prim and proper. But her title made it clear that Baur—a woman working uphill in a man's world her entire life—was in charge.

Indeed, Baur was in charge of a little music school for privileged Cincinnati girls she founded in 1867. After an unexpected run of eighty-eight years, her Cincinnati Conservatory of Music merged with its rival Cincinnati College of Music, becoming a powerful magnet for worldwide musical and theater artists of all kinds. That reputation thrives today as the University of Cincinnati's College-Conservatory of Music.

CCM's student body has included opera star Kathleen Battle, Tony Award winner Faith Prince, jazz great Al Hirt and singer/television show host Tennessee Ernie Ford. These four stars and many more have Clara Baur to thank for starting something small that became so, so big.

Baur was born in 1835 and baptized a Lutheran in Württemberg, Germany. She escaped the aftermath of Germany's 1848 civil war by immigrating at fourteen to live with her brothers in Cincinnati. Initially, Baur taught private piano and voice lessons, often earning as little as $1 a day. She returned to Germany to further her music education at about age thirty.

Back in Cincinnati a year later, Baur gathered her savings, rented space at Miss Nourse's School for Young Girls in Walnut Hills and embarked on a forty-five-year career as the "directress" of a school whose foundation was "God and the study of music." She taught her specialties, voice and piano, as well as social graces, posture and language that were in line with her finishing school location.

Baur spent about fifteen years there, then in 1876, she became more visible by moving into a building at Vine and Eighth street downtown where she launched the Cincinnati Conservatory of Music brand.

And the powers that be, including male movers and shakers George Ward Nichols and Reuben Springer, took notice. Within two years, they established the Cincinnati College of Music in the brand new Music Hall.

Unfettered, Baur pressed on with success. The Conservatory's popularity had spread nationwide, and its students included children as young as age six. Baur offered diplomas to those who completed broad coursework, certificates to those who mastered a single branch of music, and testimonials to deserving short-term students.

By 1881, Baur was holding Saturday Evening Musicals that featured her faculty members and students. She also began the first summer music program in the country. In addition to leading private and public performances by her students, Baur spread her passion for music by giving talks and readings before groups such as the Cincinnati Woman's Club.

Growth of Conservatory programs, students and teaching staff required more space, which Baur found in 1888 at a Fourth and Lawrence streets mansion near the Ohio River. All of this Baur did with her own money—no endowment, no investors. In effect, she ran the Cincinnati Conservatory of Music as a non-profit.

Yet despite Baur's impact on one of the great musical centers in America, there is little physical evidence of it around the city, not even an alley bearing her name. You can, however, find it on a 1914 Clement Barnhorn-sculpted fountain in the CCM Alumni Garden and an intimate reception and student meeting room added to CCM's Corbett Center in 1999.

Both pale in comparison to the ten-acre estate of the John Shillito department store family that Baur bought in 1902 to be the new home of her students. The James W. McLaughlin-designed and Samuel Hannaford & Sons-expanded school was a Mount Auburn landmark then and for sixty-five years thereafter.

Its grounds and buildings, once a mecca for music instruction, became part of UC from 1962 to 1967, after which the estate was razed. The building on that Oak Street site now houses the Cincinnati Public Schools offices.

At its peak, the complex accommodated 1,000 students. Its landscaped paths inspired creativity and its grand rooms were pitch-perfect for music instruction. There were dormitories and studios for students as well as a 600-seat performance hall.

With these tools and the finest of faculties to mold talent, the grand conservatory elevated the lives of thousands of students and rivaled the European conservatories that Baur emulated. Competition, however, required more than running a school. Baur spread the word of her revered Conservatory by advertising in national publications.

One ad touted CCM's broad scope of courses: "pianoforte, voice culture, pipe organ, cabinet organ, violin, violoncello, flute, cornet and other orchestral instruments, theory of music, ensemble playing, elocution, and physical culture; also, modern languages, and English literature."

As the school's reputation spread, so did the fame of its guests. A June 1962 *Cincinnati Enquirer* article about the school's sale to UC recalled that "Pablo Cassals and Fritz Kreisler have walked its ornamented floors. The voice of Enrico Caruso has sounded through its lofty rooms."

Throughout her life in her "dream" job, Baur lived modestly and unmarried in various places in Cincinnati, sometimes with a brother or friends from Germany. Her niece, Bertha, was her constant companion and business partner. Bertha took over as the conservatory's leadership duties when her aunt died in 1912 and carried on the Baur musical mission until her own death in 1940.

Both women put music before anything, especially money. The self-sacrificing Baurs never accepted salaries, possibly because "they were afraid some ambitious young man or young woman might be deprived of the opportunity to study music," wrote Lewis A. Leonard in his 1927 book *Greater Cincinnati and Its People.*

Clara Baur's style and achievements received international notice, as well. *The World Almanac & Book of Facts* wrote in its 1906 edition that her "courage, pluck and knowledge...proved a better foundation for enduring success than an endowment fund" and contributed "a signal part in the development of musical culture in America."

Clara and Bertha Baur are buried side-by-side at Spring Grove Cemetery.

XI

Richard Clayton

Publicity fanned first balloonist's fame

Let's go back sixty-eight years before the Wright Brothers' 1903 flight at Kitty Hawk, North Carolina. In 1835, Richard Clayton, English watchmaker and silversmith, became a national and international sensation by flying his hydrogen gas-fueled balloon, *Star of the West*, for nine and a half hours and 350 miles from downtown Cincinnati before crashing into a tree and falling asleep against its trunk in Virginia.

Clayton was the first to see Cincinnati, whose population was about 40,000 at the time, and the Ohio River from any higher than the top of a hill. In doing so, he set time and distance world records for "aeronauts," as nineteenth century balloonists were called.

His journey was a spectacle.

Early balloonists were of two persuasions: scientists and entertainers. Clayton was the latter, like P.T. Barnum before America knew who Phineas Taylor was.

Clayton, twenty-eight and three years older than Barnum, made and sold watches and coin silver wares from Clayton's Wholesale House at Second and Sycamore streets. He put catchy advertisements of his pending flight in local newspapers and sold tickets through hotels to those who desired to watch his "grand aerial voyage, in the most splendid balloon in the U.S." Tickets to the inaugural launch of the fifty-foot-high *Star of the West* from a Court Street platform cost fifty cents (about $11.50 in today's currency).

What a sight it must have been. Although the balloon could carry 1,000 pounds, Clayton boarded it with just a single passenger: a twenty-pound dog. The *Star of the West* lifted off at 5 p.m. on April 8 and ascended to the altitude of about a mile before Clayton—forever the showman—tossed the dog overboard. The crowd must have gasped simultaneously as the dog hurtled downward before—surprise!—a parachute opened to carry the pup to a safe landing.

How far and exactly where Clayton intended to fly his balloon isn't known—probably as far as the wind and the balloon's 4,500 square feet of sturdy silk could take him. That turned out to be a 3,000-foot mountain, a virtually uninhabited place called Keeney's Knob (near present-day Alderson, West Virgina).

Star of the West landed safely in a tree at roughly 2:30 a.m. on April 9. After sleeping until sunrise, he climbed to the top of the knob, looked down into a river valley and must have thought, "Where there is a river, there is civilization," and he set out to find help.

He found it. Locals helped Clayton locate his damaged balloon on the second day of their search. They packaged the *Star* up and took it and Clayton to the Ohio River, where he boarded a steamboat downriver to his home. Cincinnatians greeted their hero with great enthusiasm.

The Cincinnati Aviation Heritage Society set the scene: "People came for miles to view this strange unheard of monster of the air. Many thought it impossible to make the trip from Cincinnati in nine hours, and condemned the whole story as a fake."

It was no fake. It was the beginning of an aeronautical career that Clayton, the great balloonist of the West, pursued for at least ten years before returning full-time to his business, aptly renamed Clayton's Balloon Store.

Few details of Clayton's personal life can be found on history websites. He was born in England in 1807, and the aeronautical technology first introduced successfully by French aeronauts in 1783 fascinated the young Clayton. The hot-air balloon craze came to America in 1793, when President George Washington witnessed a flight. Clayton didn't arrive in the United States until the early 1830s, choosing the western outpost of Cincinnati as his home.

Yearning to one-up New England aeronauts, Clayton built the *Star of the West*. He followed up his record flight with several others, but gusty winds during a May flight forced him to land on a Cincinnati rooftop, damaging the *Star* beyond repair.

On July 4, in a new balloon financed by fans and friends, Clayton delivered the first unofficial air mail package in United States history with a flight aimed at the Atlantic Ocean. Freezing temperatures and leaks in his balloon forced him to abort the flight. He landed safely and deposited the mail after walking to a post office in Waverly, south of Chillicothe, Ohio. Another 1835 flight ended when his balloon exploded, but its silk acted as a parachute, and Clayton was unharmed.

He made about a dozen other flights, taking off from cities such as New Orleans, Pittsburgh, Lexington and Louisville. The press covered his exploits, and he often wrote letters to editors that they published. Being the first person to see Louisville from the air, Clayton described to the press what he saw shortly after taking off from that city on August 16, 1837:

My situation now was truly delightful, I could sit at ease and view the city and its thousands of inhabitants who were collected in groups in streets and on the tops of buildings. I could see the ferry boat and other steamboats puffing along, and I could clearly see and hear the Falls of the Ohio River.

Clayton owned Somerset Hall, part of an 1845 estate built by Southern plantation slaves in Ludlow, Kentucky, that earned state historic landmark status in 2014. The 1860 census listed him as a retired merchant living with a fifteen-year-old girl, possibly his daughter, named Charlotte. No wife was listed, but his personal and real estate wealth was estimated to be $100,000 (more than $2.6 million today).

What became of Clayton after 1860 is unclear. Louis Daguerre's photographic technique, first available in 1839, had arrived in Cincinnati, but a published image of Clayton could not be found. West Virginians, however, did not forget him. An unincorporated community near his landing spot bears his name: Clayton, West Virgina.

Remnants of Clayton's life such as a signed watch or a silver spoon or fork pop up in online auctions. Treasured antiques bearing the image of the *Star of the West* in flight exist, as well. Two of them, a commemorative bandbox and a stoneware jug, were exhibited at the Cincinnati Art Museum in 2014.

Kitaro Shirayamadani

Japanese potter gleamed in art's golden era

Few Cincinnatians had ever seen anyone like twenty-two-year-old Kitaro Shirayamadani when he arrived in the Queen City in 1887 to throw and decorate ceramics for Rookwood Pottery. In fact, it is likely he was the first Japanese man to make Cincinnati his home.

Shirayamadani's impeccable pots featured silver overlay, realistic and exquisitely painted serpents, fish, birds, flowers and other aesthetic images in a style straight out of Japan and of a quality few American potters had achieved. He was the seventh decorator hired by Maria Longworth Storer to work at the pottery she founded seven years earlier. His Rookwood career spanned its golden, pre-Depression era and beyond until his death in 1948 at age eighty-three. (Some sources say he was ninety, others ninety-seven, possibly because the artist was known to fib about his age.)

Shirayamadani's greatness peaked in 2004 when Cincinnati Art Galleries auctioned one of his pots for $350,750, the most ever paid for a piece of Rookwood pottery and a record likely to stand forever.

Despite his fifty-plus years at Rookwood (taking eight years off to return to Japan in the 1910s), little is known about how "Shiri" or "Sherry" as he was called, became such a great painter/potter. It's also unclear what kind of person he was, possibly because he kept to himself, concentrated on perfecting his pottery and feeding a pet mouse in his attic studio at Rookwood's Mount Adams factory.

There is but one telling newspaper article about Shirayamadani in the archives at the Public Library of Cincinnati and Hamilton County. It is short and quotes the great artist just once. Wrote *Cincinnati Post* reporter Eugene Segal in 1936 after visiting Shiri in his studio:

It is hard to imagine that he has a home. One receives the impression that he is there always, painting the delicate flowers and pastel backgrounds which characterize his work.... Long as he has been at the pottery, none of his associates know much about him.

Shirayamadani revealed little about himself when questioned by Segal. Asked to tell the story of how he learned to paint, Shiri answered that he learned at school and at work. "I was a boy," he told Segal. He revealed no source of his talent or his motivation to adopt a foreign city whose people likely saw him as a curiosity.

Nevertheless, that young, lone Japanese man grew into an American star in a hurry. William Watts Taylor, who joined Rookwood in 1883 and guided it to greatness after Storer slipped into the background, promoted Shiri in national advertisements after the artist made his public debut at the October 1887 Piedmont Exhibition in Atlanta. He had been at Rookwood for just five months.

It was the dream of Storer—a huge fan of Asian art whose own pots often were rough interpretations of it—to make "Japanese Rookwood." Shiri made that dream come true.

"He could do everything," said art pottery expert and former Cincinnati auction gallery director Riley Humler, who coordinated the sale the day Shirayamadani's pot set the Rookwood record. "The only criticism you hear is that he lived so long his work got a little sloppy."

Shirayamadani's valuable pots have made a lot of collectors and auctioneers very happy. And his role as an ambassador for Rookwood came to the fore when the company sent him to Japan to present three pots to Prime Minister Ito Hirobumi, who was "greatly interested in his work," the *Cincinnati Enquirer* reported in May 1902. Where seemingly shy Shiri derived the moxie to meet such a challenge is unknown. Yet he returned to Japan in 1912—some historians say he worked for the Imperial government—in tumultuous political times before and during World War I.

Kitaro Shirayama (he added the "dani") was born to a samurai family in Kanazawa, Ishikawa Prefecture, Japan, in 1865. His first name means "man of love and joy" and his last name means "White Mountain Valley," referring to his birthplace in west-central Honshu. Why he added "dani" to his name is unclear. Roughly, it translates to English as "tick," but it could also represent "tiny" or "small." Either way, his was a tongue-twister of a name—SHEER-ah-YAH-mah-DAH-nee—and made him seem bigger than his slight stature.

His first contact with Cincinnati came in September 1886 when the porcelain decorator demonstrated his art at the Cincinnati Industrial Exposition, a type of world's fair event held in and around Washington Park. He was one of about one hundred Japanese in the expo's Japanese Village, but apparently he was the one who caught Storer's eye. She lured him away from his job in the curio shop Fujiyama in Boston the following May and set Shirayamadani up in a boarding house with another Rookwood decorator.

City records show that, in the years to follow, the sweet and highly cultured artist boarded in several dwellings within walking distance of Rookwood Pottery, which overlooked downtown Cincinnati from Mount Adams. (The timbered building exists but hasn't been a pottery since 1959.) He molded unique ceramic shapes and decorated them in a greatly detailed, West-meets-East style on all sides, not just one like most of his contemporaries. His works inspired many potters to emulate him.

Americans' unfamiliarity with Japanese names has led to numerous mispronunciations of his last name. And documented misspellings of his first name included Ketaro, Katarro, Ketara, Retaro and Kewaro. The art pottery world misspells his name Kataro to this day.

Shirayamadani suffered a head wound when he fell down fifteen steps en route to a television filming at Rookwood Pottery in 1947. He contracted a severe cold the next year and had been hospitalized for two weeks before he died on July 19, 1948. The official cause of Shirayamadani's death was "coronary thrombosis," according to records at Spring Grove Cemetery, where he was buried in a cement vault under a modest ground marker.

On that marker, the great ceramicist's name is spelled correctly, K-i-t-a-r-o.

Mary Greene

First female captain ran big rivers

In her lifetime (1867–1949), Mary Greene might have been described as a "great gal" who succeeded in a "man's world." But more than seven decades after her death, with women's history in sharper focus and political correctness the norm, the first woman to captain steamboats on the Ohio and Mississippi rivers can be called nothing less than an "American legend."

Greater Cincinnatian Tom Greene experienced both the "then" and the "now" of his grandmother's legend. But as one who ran the decks of the family's famed *Delta Queen* passenger steamboat as a little boy, he sees her through purely nostalgic eyes.

"She was a grand lady...a wonderful grandma," Tom said in a 2017 interview. "She was always gracious, just a very lovely lady."

Blue-eyed Mary Greene, though short in stature, was also tough. Turning the wheel of the *Argand* through an Ohio River cyclone to safe harbor took strength. Bolstering her family business, Greene Line Steamers, by buying out its competition took moxie.

The legend of Mary Greene's fifty-seven years on steamboats was a national one. Following her death in the spring of 1949 at age eighty-one, *TIME* magazine published a short obituary on page seventy-nine about her ambitious and amazing life as well as her soft side. "A good housewife who spent her free time embroidering, she raised a family on the boats as they plied up and down the river between Pittsburgh, Cincinnati and New Orleans."

If *TIME* had more space, oh how much more of Mary's unique life it could have printed! Tom Greene said he best remembers his grandmother living on the *Gordon C. Greene* later in life when her son, Greene's father

Tom, was its captain. She was an avid dancer and would sprinkle the cabin's floor with flakes of soap to make stepping out to Big Band music easier, the younger Greene said.

He remembers fondly that Mary would shoo him away from the adults on "Grab Bag" nights. When the band stopped playing, Mary would invite guests to choose a small bag of trinkets she had laid out on a card table. After seeing what they had, passengers were asked to write a little poem about their trip on the *Gordon C. Greene*, or about a favored crew member or a friend they had made onboard.

"A lot of people would write about Grandma," her grandson said. "They were always very complimentary. When they read them, she'd sit up and politely smile."

Yes, in her later years, Captain Mary Greene had given up the wheel and become Hostess Mary Greene. She danced on the *Gordon C. Greene* the last night she entertained there. She began feeling ill in the next days and stayed in Cincinnati at Tom's family house.

"She slept in the big middle room upstairs," recalled Tom. "She slept in the one bed, which was a double bed. I slept in the same bed the last night of her life." Mary was able to return to her number 24 room on the *Delta Queen*, which was moored at the foot of Main Street. Soon thereafter, she died of a heart attack on April 22, 1949.

"It was fitting," Tom said. According to her obituary in the *Cincinnati Times-Star*, Mary often sang this ditty: "If you ride behind two stacks, you're doomed to ride aboard a steamboat until you're tombed."

Mary Elizabeth Becker was born on an Ohio River island outside Marietta, Ohio. Her father was a shopkeeper, and she had three brothers and a sister. Mary married Gordon Christopher Greene, a riverboat pilot, in Marietta in 1890, and she learned to steer his steamer, the *H.K. Bedford*, on their honeymoon. The couple doubled the size of Greene Line Steamers four years later with the purchase of the 132-foot *Argand*.

"As a result of the long hours of companionship in the pilot house, she began learning the tortuous channel, the shoals, and the bars, the obstructions hidden from the untrained eye, and the numberless things a pilot must know to steer a boat safely when the channel is narrow and treacherous," reads a 1927 article in *American Magazine.*

She became the first woman on the nation's interior waterways to earn her captain's license in 1895, passing a grueling test in Pittsburgh. She returned there to earn her master's license in 1896.

There were thousands of packet boats moving goods on the Ohio River, but Gordon and Mary steamed ahead of their competition by launching the only side-wheeler ever in the Greene Line, the 210-foot *Greenland*, in 1903. Mary captained it to the World's Fair in St. Louis in 1904, carrying freight and passengers.

She had three sons in those early days. One died as a boy. Tom, who was born on the *Greenland*, and his younger brother by three years, Chris, grew to be strapping young men and skilled captains.

Even though *American Magazine* wrote that "strength is nearly as important as skill in maneuvering a boat," little Mary commanded her boats and ran the business after Gordon died in 1927. She counted on her boys to steer the steamers a lot more after that and ran a tight but entertaining ship. *Cincinnati Post* columnist Robert C. Ruark wrote in 1948 that "No Mississippi gamblers ride Ma Greene's craft, and there is no carousing on a run that used to be a ripsnorter. Captain Greene sells no hard licker on her boat."

At the peak of its sixty-plus years of operation, Greene Line Steamers had about twenty-five boats on the Ohio. The Greenes launched their passenger line in 1935 with the purchase of the twenty-two-year-old steamer *Cape Giradeau*. Mary honored her late husband by renaming it the *Gordon C. Greene*, which became Mary's home on the river. The Greenes also bought the *Delta Queen*, which became a Cincinnati symbol for decades.

Mary Greene is buried next to her husband in Newport Cemetery, sixteen miles upriver from Marietta. But her spirit lingers in the form of a statue in Covington, Kentucky's George Rogers Park. She stands there today, at a big steamboat wheel, facing north across Riverside Drive and her beloved Ohio River toward the Cincinnati skyline.

Samuel Hannaford

Landmark architect rebelled and excelled

Had Samuel Hannaford signed his art like a painter or sculptor, his name would be all over buildings in Greater Cincinnati, among them City Hall, Music Hall and dozens of grand homes.

Arguably the region's most famous architect and certainly its most prolific in the late 1800s and early 1900s, Hannaford and his sons, Harvey and Charles, left their mark by designing more than sixty structures listed on the National Register of Historic Places. Dozens more were razed.

Look for the Hannaford name around Cincinnati, however, and you won't see it often. A one-block street in Norwood, a motel in Kenwood, an 1890s apartment building in old Newport, a playground in Spring Grove Village and a cocktail lounge in Covington sport the Hannaford name.

Samuel Hannaford's impressive professional career is well documented, but his private life is less so. A good account is an eScrapbook piece compiled by Betty Ann Smiddy. The historian chronicles how Samuel was the third born in a family of eleven children who toiled on a farm in Widdecombe-on-the-Moor, Devonshire, England, until hard times drove them to the United States in 1844.

"The family lived downtown for several months before buying a thirty-eight-and-a-half-acre farm in Cheviot for $4,000," Smiddy wrote. Young Samuel attended private school and then Farmer's College before having a religious disagreement with his Presbyterian father and striking out on his own.

An apprenticeship with architect John Hamilton and marriage into a prominent Methodist family placed Hannaford on a successful path from which he never strayed. In 1857, he joined the architectural firm of William Tinsley and Edwin Anderson, with whom he likely designed the oldest surviving example of his residential work, the Marcus Fechheimer House at 22 Garfield Place, downtown.

When the Civil War ended in 1865, Hannaford built the home he would die in on one and a half acres at the corner of Winton Road and Derby Avenue in the newly-platted suburb of Spring Grove. The two-story, wood-sided house still stands, and the initials "SH" still show under its gables.

According to *Cincinnati: A Guide to the Queen City and Its Neighbors*, by the Federal Writers' Project, the house was built with "ten rooms with large central halls dividing west and east wings. Second floor mantel carved by William Fry. Crystal chandelier with 370 pendants in parlor. Cherry woodwork. Two marble mantels trimmed in New England marble."

On Derby, the Hannafords reared two boys and a girl. Samuel's first wife died in 1871, but he remarried and had four more children, two of whom died in infancy. His second wife died in 1883, but he married a third time to a much younger woman who bore him three more children.

Hannaford, Smiddy wrote, was committed deeply to his community, which adopted the name Winton Place in 1882 and made him its first and final mayor. (Cincinnati annexed the village in 1903, and it is Spring Grove Village today.) He was president of the school board for many years and a leader of his neighborhood's Methodist Episcopal congregation, for whom he designed a church in 1884 that still stands.

As mayor, Hannaford was a Republican who had a sincere interest in creating a healthy environment for his neighbors, many of whom were family. A 1902 report by the Ohio State Board of Health shows that Hannaford, whose first wife likely died of typhoid fever contracted from contaminated drinking water, proposed a trunk sewer be built to reduce waste dumped into nearby Mill Creek.

The "water of Mill Creek is fearfully foul and is growing more so every passing year; in fact during the summer time Mill Creek is one long drawn out 'stink.' " Hannaford wrote in a letter to a state health board member. Winton Place began accepting bids for the project the following year.

Hannaford also was concerned with air quality in the industrial Mill Creek Valley. He badgered City Hall officials for not enforcing pollution laws. Said Hannaford in a July 1902 article in the *Cincinnati Enquirer*: "It is a shameful injustice yet one that goes on year after year by default of city officials to do their duty." He said he believed that seventy-five percent of the "sooty impurities" that spewed from "persons using power boilers" could be prevented.

Clearly, Hannaford was part of a progressive movement sweeping the land as the populace complained about the negative impacts the Industrial Revolution was having on land and people. The 1919 book *Memoirs of the Miami Valley, Vol. 3* by John C. Hover and Joseph D. Barnes, describes the architect: "Mr. Hannaford was an honest, upright man, firm in his convictions and fearless in adhering to them. He was one of the most loyal and public-spirited of Cincinnati's pioneers, and all during his life was eager to co-operate in the movements for the public good."

Samuel Hannaford retired from his architectural firm in 1904 and had a stroke in 1909. He would die two years later. His funeral was held in the Methodist church he designed, and he was buried at Spring Grove Cemetery across Winton Road from his home. At his request, no stone marks his grave.

It is estimated that in the twenty years Samuel Hannaford worked independently and more than fifteen years he worked with his sons, he had his hands on the drawings of more than 300 buildings in Hamilton County. Here is a short list of Hannaford-designed buildings standing in Greater Cincinnati: Cincinnati City, Music and Memorial halls; Clifton Branch Library; The Phoenix, downtown; Old St. George Church, Corryville; Sorg mansion and Opera House, Middletown; Eden Park Water Tower; Wiedemann Mansion, Newport; The Precinct restaurant, Columbia Tusculum; Twin Towers, College Hill; Norman Chapel, Spring Grove Cemetery; Hamilton County Jobs and Family Services building, Over-the-Rhine; Cincinnati Observatory, Mount Lookout; and the Brittany and Lombardy apartments, downtown.

LIBBY HOLMAN

Broadway singer rode roller-coaster life

Had Libby Holman—accused murderer, Broadway star, torch singer, open bisexual and friend of Montgomery Clift, Dorothy Parker, and Martin Luther King Jr.—graduated from the University of Cincinnati in 2013 instead of 1923, she would have been a YouTube and tabloid sensation.

Vivacious, outrageous, courageous, intelligent and on the crest of America's cultural curve, Holman told a friend upon becoming the youngest woman to graduate from UC at nineteen that she would be a star and marry a rich man—and she did. But hers was an extremely bumpy ride, one that is documented in numerous articles and in great detail in Jon Bradshaw's 1985 biography *Dreams That Money Can Buy: The Tragic Life of Libby Holman.*

Bradshaw describes Holman's "madcap career" and how it "toppled into ruin." He takes you to a fateful night in August 1932 when an intoxicated Libby told her husband, R.J. Reynolds Tobacco Co. heir Zachary Smith Reynolds, that she was pregnant. Bradshaw describes how they likely argued and how a bullet allegedly fired by Holman killed Reynolds. Press coverage ran on page one of *The New York Times* several times but disappeared after charges were dropped with the Reynolds family's approval.

Holman went on to appear in more than ten Broadway musicals, charted four Top 20 hits—including her signature song, "Moanin' Low"—and ended her career by performing two concerts at the United Nations in New York. She ran with a who's-who crowd that included Parker, H.L. Mencken, Noel Coward, Richard Rodgers, Lorenz Hart and Gertrude Lawrence.

Success did not make her rich, but her son's inheritance did. With it, she built a thirty-room Georgian mansion on 110 acres in Connecticut where she entertained progressive-thinking celebrities such as Elizabeth Taylor, Tennessee Williams, Tallulah Bankhead, Truman Capote, Imogene Coca, Martha Raye and Roddy McDowell.

But her life was deeply scarred by the disappearance of two uncles, the suicide of another uncle and her estranged second husband, the 1950 mountain climbing accident that killed her only biological son and the mysterious 1966 death of Clift, who was one of many gay men and women Holman loved.

In the end, the Cincinnati woman whose family ironically nicknamed her "Baby" couldn't take any more tragedy. According to UC archivist Kevin Grace's 2001 book, *Legendary Locals of Cincinnati*, on June 18, 1971, at the age of sixty-seven, "Libby Holman put on a bathing suit, sat in her garaged Rolls Royce, started the engine and committed suicide."

These chapters of Holman's life unfolded after she left Cincinnati for Broadway in 1924. What happened before is fodder for armchair psychologists and historians.

Elizabeth Lloyd Holzman was born to German-Jewish parents Alfred and Rachel in their spacious Walnut Hills home in late May 1904. Her father was a successful stockbroker in business with his twin brother Ross. Libby's sister, Marion, was two years older, and a brother, Alfred Jr., a few years younger.

One of her uncles, Charles Holzman, had run away and disappeared at age sixteen. Facing theft and embezzlement charges that dogged Alfred for the rest of his life, Ross ran off in 1905. Bradshaw wrote that Libby was fascinated by Ross, who was dapper and silver-tongued with a seductive smile, swagger and goal of becoming a millionaire.

Life for the Holzmans went downhill after Ross vanished. Alfred covered about $250,000 in debts Ross had tied to the family business. Libby's father sold the family home in 1908, moving into a small apartment in the Avondale neighborhood. Libby shared a room with Marion. Alfred Jr. slept in the dining room, and their "mightily mean" mother ran the household, according to Bradshaw.

Libby entered kindergarten at Avondale School in 1909. She played the role of Puck in the school's rendition of *A Midsummer Night's Dream* and was so precocious she skipped two grades. A childhood tonsillectomy made her voice deep and throaty and became her signature.

Olive-skinned with raven hair, Libby longed to be a blonde and began to exhibit a special type of individualism early on. She was just eleven years old when her beloved uncle Wallace, a superintendent of a downtown distributorship and father of three, killed himself.

Libby was profoundly affected by the loss of a third uncle, but she persevered and entered Hughes High School at age twelve, two years after World War II broke out in Europe. Being of German heritage suddenly became worse than being Jewish, which she disdained. Anti-German hysteria was widespread.

Libby blossomed, however, when Alfred took the "z" out of the family name. When a senior at fifteen, Libby Holman was far from a classic beauty but was considered by Hughes boys to be "hot stuff," Bradshaw wrote. She graduated high school three weeks after her sixteenth birthday in June 1920. The Hughes Annual named her the "nerviest" senior, adding that "We all expect to see Libby before the footlights someday."

At UC, she smoked cigarettes, bobbed her hair, and wore heavy makeup, revealing clothes and a rakishly angled fedora. In her third year, Holman played "an aesthetic flapper" in a racy campus comedy called *Fresh Paint*. Critics adored her but said her singing was more impassioned than good. She graduated with high grades a month into her twentieth year.

Holman stuck around UC after graduation, honing her theater skills and shedding her stage inhibitions by walking naked among friends. She debarked for New York in June 1924 and landed her first Broadway role the following year, launching a career whose peaks and valleys mirrored her childhood.

She returned to Cincinnati on occasion to visit her sister and go to the theater, but soon Broadway stopped calling, and her singing career waned. She spent her time rearing two adopted boys, championing civil rights and entertaining her famous friends at the Connecticut mansion she called Treetops, where she planned "to live to be a smart old witch who rules her kingdom with an iron scepter."

Libby Holman's colorful story might have turned gray, but online videos keep her throaty voice alive.

Robert Duncanson

Painter-abolitionist impacted all races

Revered landscape painter Robert S. Duncanson—the first African American to earn an international reputation in the fine arts world—seemingly moved with ease between the white and Black societies of Cincinnati in the mid-1800s.

Photographs show he was a far better dresser than his benefactor, eccentric Cincinnati multimillionaire Nicholas Longworth. Duncanson had light brown skin and combed his hair tight to his scalp, helping him fit in with whites for whom he painted portraits and sweeping landscapes.

But there was another side to Duncanson: He was an abolitionist.

In 1855, African-American photographer James Presley Ball of Cincinnati fielded a team from the nation's first cluster of Black artists to create a 2,500-square-yard mural depicting the horrors of slavery. Ball's friend, Duncanson, provided counsel and served as his touch-up artist.

Duncanson (1821–1872) lived and worked in fast-growing Cincinnati, then a center of abolitionism. The Anti-Slavery League so admired the artist that it paid him to travel to Europe to study with the masters. Duncanson also participated in anti-slavery societies and donated paintings to raise them money.

It took a special person to walk the line between the races, but walk it he did—for a lifetime.

Art critics Everlyn Nicodemus and Kristian Romare wrote this about Duncanson in their essay "Africa in Scotland, Scotland in Africa:" "The unforeseeable play of genes had supplied Robert Duncanson with a fairly light complexion. He could have passed for being white. But African American he was, and he was widely known as such in Cincinnati through his collaboration with fellow African Americans and abolitionists."

Duncanson's great-grandfather was a Scotsman and a slaveholder in Virginia. A son he fathered with a slave grew up to be the plantation's house painter, who earned enough money to buy his freedom and escape to the North with his family. Robert's father, John Duncanson, married Lucy Nichols and had seven children in upstate New York and Canada, where they would be safe from slave hunters.

When the family moved west to Michigan, Robert was about ten and first saw the Hudson River, whose school of painters he emulated later in life. Drama and courage came into Duncanson's life in Michigan. He broke off from his father while in his late teens and started a house painting company, taking out ads in local papers to build his business. In addition, he painted portraits with "stereotypical stiffness," wrote Nicodemus and Romare. But the self-taught artist kept at it and started painting landscapes.

In about 1840 and estranged from his angry father, Duncanson moved to a community of abolitionists and free Black men north of Cincinnati called Mount Pleasant (later renamed Mount Healthy). He copied prints, worked in photography and landed his first exhibit of Hudson River School-style landscapes in 1842. Duncanson married during this period and had a son, Reuben. But his wife, Rebecca Graham, died, leaving him alone with the baby. Census records show he remarried a much younger woman named Phoebe but probably not until the mid-1850s at the earliest.

Duncanson got his big break in 1851. Wealthy winemaker and abolitionist Nicholas Longworth, at one time the nation's second biggest tax payer behind John Jacob Astor, hired Duncanson to paint murals on the entry hall walls of Belmont, the family's downtown estate that is the Taft Museum of Art today.

"When [Longworth] gave Duncanson this very important commission, he gave him the Good Housekeeping stamp of approval," wrote Smithsonian Institution art historian Claire Perry. The Belmont murals helped earn the ambitious Duncanson his first trip to Europe in 1853.

The outbreak of the Civil War, followed by the Emancipation Proclamation, instilled fear in the North, including Cincinnati. Tumultuous times tainted attitudes toward free Blacks, and some historians theorize that a worried Duncanson, who now had a second son, left Cincinnati for a few years.

He traveled to Canada and reconnected with the art community there. Then he was off to Europe, where he was treated like a celebrity. He met earls, duchesses, even the King of Sweden, who purchased his celebrated painting, "Land of the Lotus Eaters." Even Queen Victoria bought a Duncanson painting, according to www.findagrave.com.

The last half of the 1860s were Duncanson's peak years as a landscape artist. He opened a gallery in Cincinnati, painted views of his beloved Scottish Highlands and toured the states, selling paintings for as much as $15,000 (about $300,000 in today's currency).

But something was wrong with Robert Duncanson. He became delusional and fitful, and art historians say his paintings reflected turbulent mood swings. What caused his declining behavior is not clear. One theory is that it was lead poisoning contracted over decades of painting houses, mixing paints and creating art. Or could it have been the stress of constantly straddling white and Black societies?

"He did live a life of incredible stress as a successful African American in a white-dominated world," wrote the Smithsonian's Perry. "But people who perform at the highest level of artistic skills are also people of unusual sensitivity."

Robert Duncanson died in October 1872 two months after suffering a seizure while setting up an exhibition in Detroit. He is buried in an unmarked grave in his boyhood home of Monroe, Michigan.

Eight of Duncanson's trompe l'oeil murals in the Taft Museum of Art "stand as the most accomplished domestic mural paintings in America before the Civil War," according to art historian Joseph D. Ketner II. Yet like the man who took two years to complete them with paint he mixed himself, the murals were quickly forgotten, papered over before Duncanson died.

The murals were rediscovered behind layers of wallpaper in 1930 and restored in 2004. Today, the sweeping scenes are a key attraction at the Taft Museum and closely guarded. In 1986, the museum created the Duncanson Artist-in-Residence program to spotlight top African-American painters, photographers, musicians, dancers, authors, poets and other artists from around the country. His work and his legacy endure in Cincinnati.

James Presley Ball

Portrait photographer embraced diversity

Queen Victoria, Charles Dickens, Frederick Douglass, Jenny Lind. James Presley Ball—a free Black man, traveler, politician, family-focused entrepreneur and owner of a classy gallery in downtown Cincinnati—photographed them all.

Ball (1825–1904), however, was far more than a photographer to the famous. He elevated American culture by recording the images of children, Blacks and whites, the poor and the privileged—even the dead—at a time in American history when an increasingly dispersed, diverse and faster-paced population desired an inexpensive way to document friends, families and departed loved ones.

Daguerreotype photography was new technology when Ball set up his studio in 1849. He was one of about thirty photographers in town, but he stood out as a popular and affordable choice.

Not to be forgotten, as Ball was for many decades after his death, is the fact that he was an outspoken abolitionist, who, in 1855, assembled a crew of African-American artists, which included Cincinnati landscape painter Robert Duncanson, to create a 2,500-square-yard mural on canvas of paneled imagery that conveyed the horrors of slavery.

What happened to the mural is a mystery, but a fifty-six-page pamphlet with abolitionist Achilles Pugh's descriptions of it survives under the title *Ball's Splendid Mammoth Pictorial of the United States, Comprising Views of the African Slave Trade; of Northern and Southern Cities; of Cotton and Sugar Plantations; of the Mississippi, Ohio and Susquehanna Rivers, Niagara Falls, & C.*

Ball first showed the mural in Cincinnati at the Ohio Mechanics Institute in March 1855. He charged ten to thirty cents per viewer, but he held benefit showings for children, churches and families who could not afford admission. Boston also hosted a showing of the mural, after which its whereabouts went undocumented.

Also missing are the portraits Ball made of Queen Victoria and Dickens, the existence of which were reported in the *London Times*. And despite the thousands of exposures he made over a fifty-year career, only one is known to exist of the great photographer.

Taken when Ball was in his seventies, the daguerreotype image shows the profile of a light-skinned African American dressed in a fine suit and tie, sporting a long, bushy beard that was in fashion for much of his life. He looks successful and much like the patriarch he was to his brother, with whom he worked in Cincinnati, and his children, with whom he worked and lived until his 1904 death in Honolulu.

James Presley Ball was born to William and Susan Ball, who likely were free Virginians. He learned photography in White Sulphur Springs, West Virginia, from John B. Bailey, an African American from Boston. At twenty, Ball opened a one-room daguerreotype studio in Cincinnati, but it didn't succeed, so he took his fledgling career elsewhere around Ohio and to cities such as Pittsburgh and Richmond, Virginia.

Historians speculate Ball might have been drawn back to the Queen City in 1849 because it had a growing community of Black artists and a fiercely outspoken group of abolitionists led by Lyman Beecher, Calvin Stowe, Levi Coffin and Pugh.

The 1850 Census shows Ball, his parents and younger siblings, Thomas and Lizzie, living together in Cincinnati's 9th Ward, northeast of Central Parkway (then the Miami-Erie Canal) in the Pendleton neighborhood. Ball married a Mississippian named Virginia in about 1850, and they had four daughters and a son. In the 1870 Census, the names of Virginia and daughter Victoria don't appear, suggesting they had died.

Business boomed for Ball, and within several years he settled into an expansive space at 28 W. Fourth St., which he named the Great Daguerrean Gallery of the West. He employed as many as nine people, among them his brother, his brother-in-law Alexander Thomas, and the painter Duncanson.

A Cincinnati neighbor, Eliza Potter, described Ball's gallery in her 1859 tell-all book *A Hairdresser's Experience in High Life*: "The photographer J.P. Ball, who owns a magnificent daguerrean gallery, has a reputation that is known in nearly every State of the Union, and he has displayed on the walls of his gallery several of the finest landscapes painted by the accomplished artist Robert Duncanson."

Ball exhibited his photographs throughout the 1850s at the Ohio Mechanics Institute. He opened a second gallery and partnered with his brother-in-law. While in Europe for six months, he photographed Queen Victoria, who hung the portrait in her boudoir. While in England, he and Virginia had a child named Victoria.

Ball photographed the family of Ulysses S. Grant, as well. This "indicated the respect which prominent Cincinnatians held for Ball...whether out of sympathy for African Americans generally, and/or because of Ball's skill, location, impressive business, and affordability, all factors he frequently touted in local newspapers," wrote University of Cincinnati professor Theresa Leininger-Miller.

Ball's successful career in Cincinnati ended after fifteen years. Business speculations hurt Ball & Thomas between 1865 and 1871, when the gallery's assets were liquidated. Ball left Cincinnati and returned to itinerant photography at age forty-six. His railroad route traversed Mississippi, Louisiana, Missouri, Minnesota and Montana, where he lived during much of the 1890s.

Somewhere along the way, Ball, who had written at least one anti-slavery pamphlet before, caught a bug for civic action and politics. He founded Montana's Afro-American Club, co-founded the St. James AME Church in Helena and ran for office. He didn't win, but in 1894, Ball became a Montana delegate to the National Republican Convention.

The turn of the century found Ball moving to Seattle, where his lawyer son had opened Globe Studio in 1892 and Ball & Sons studio in 1897. Rheumatism disabled Ball, and he sought relief with a daughter in Hawaii but died at seventy-nine in Hawaii on May 4, 1904. Reportedly, his cremains were returned to his surviving family in Cincinnati.

Nearly 300 of Ball's photographs, only eight of which are of African Americans, can be viewed at library.cincymuseum.org.

Carl Wiedemann

Brewing heir exploited his silver spoon

Carl Wiedemann had a famous name but led an infamous life. The grandson of Newport, Kentucky, beer magnate George Wiedemann served two years in federal prison during Prohibition for selling beer to his notorious partner, George "King of the Bootleggers" Remus. During his 1928 trial for Volstead Act violations, Wiedemann wrecked his car while driving drunk.

The American press ate up Wiedemann's wild life, dubbing him "The Playboy of the Tracks." There were many reasons.

Two of Wiedemann's many love interests jumped or "fell" from windows to their deaths. The first did it late at night when he was the only other person in her Lexington, Kentucky, hotel room. That story made the papers from the *Kentucky Post* to *The New York Times*.

Wiedemann, who for a time was a successful racehorse owner, used Kentucky Derby winnings to pay for construction of an in-ground swimming pool and a pool house at the family's mansion in Newport's Cote Brilliante neighborhood. And—surprise!—he did it unbeknownst to his kin, who were vacationing in Europe at the time.

Carl was born in Cincinnati in 1892 and grew up in the Wiedemann Mansion with little resistance from life, enjoying the finer things and the assistance of Chinese servants. According to *The Encyclopedia of Northern Kentucky*, Carl attended Yale University after training for—but being let go by—the United States Army. From 1916 to 1918, he played tackle on the Yale University football team.

Older than most students—he entered the Ivy League college as a twenty-four-year-old—he was often seen on dates with a Broadway actress. Carl denied being engaged to Allyn King, a teenage performer with a Florenz Ziegfeld review. In 1930, when King's career was more or less over, she jumped from the fifth-floor window of her aunt's New York apartment. Her death, with Wiedemann's marriage woes mixed in, made the *Times*.

The massive Wiedemann brewery in downtown Newport stabled 150 delivery horses at its peak, which perhaps inspired Carl's love of ponies. He owned twenty racehorses by 1921 and stabled them in Lexington. Following a day at Keeneland Race Course with friends, including Dorothy Rainey, whom a newspaper called "the prettiest girl in Newport," Carl prepared for a late night out with the guys. First, however, he visited Rainey's Lafayette Hotel room.

The two, who were rumored to be engaged, were alone. He said he was standing across the room and she was sitting on a sill when all of a sudden she fell through the open window. Carl raced to the street below, but Rainey was already dead.

A jury exonerated Wiedemann. He had told authorities that Rainey was subject to dizzy spells, according to an October 1921 *Times* article. Reports were that Wiedemann had broken up with Rainey and she was upset about racetrack gossip she had heard about her and Carl.

He was in the news again in 1923 when his fabled horse, In Memorium (named in honor of Rainey), defeated Kentucky Derby winner Zev at Latonia Race Track in Covington, earning Wiedemann $50,000 (more than $750,000 today).

A head-to-head runoff was held two weeks later at Churchill Downs. Zev won by a nose, but many in attendance said In Memorium was cheated. The judges' ruling stood, however, and Wiedemann lost a small fortune.

Two years later when he was down to five ponies, Wiedemann married Celia Dooin. Their relationship reportedly was strained, but they had one child, Carl Jr. By 1927, Wiedemann was out of the racing business and bootlegging with Remus, brewing at an annual rate of 1.5 million gallons a year behind the back of his family.

Carl's grand-nephew, Dick Wagner, said he understood the two bootleggers threw parties attended by writer F. Scott Fitzgerald, who some believe fashioned his famous Jay Gatsby character after Remus and Gatsby's mansion after the Wiedemann Mansion. Fitzgerald and Wiedemann had trained together at the Army's Camp Zachary Taylor outside of Louisville. It's possible they became friends over drinks at the city's Seelbach Hotel Oakroom.

An insider's tip about Wiedemann's brewing eventually sent the former prince of the ponies to the pokey. He was sentenced on February 8, 1928, to two years in prison and fined $10,000 (about $140,000 today). The press covered every detail of the short trial, and the *Kentucky Post* put a positive spin on his imprisonment:

There he will have a chance to realize what a mess he's made of his life—what worry he has caused his aged father, Charles, 71, who is now seriously ill—he can lay his plans to make amends when he returns home.

The *Post* wrote that Wiedemann planned to work on the prison farm to prove he could eschew the "featherbeds" he has enjoyed his whole life. Said Wiedemann: "When I am released from prison, I hope to be the man I was years ago and not what I am today....I have grown fat."

Although Wiedemann went to prison, and his ashamed father, who was also accused of bootlegging, died before serving time, not everything about Carl was sketchy, Wagner said. Carl's sister Irma, "just adored him" Wagner said. "She thought that he was better than sliced bread."

Out of prison, Wiedemann dabbled in the brewery's management, but by 1940 he was banned from it. Nary a bar or flophouse turned him away, and his family felt disgraced. Still, they gave him cash and sometimes paid his bills with beer. Eventually, the *Post* wrote, "He could be seen hob-nobbing with Newport's addicts of the underworld. He took to drink."

Carl Wiedemann died on February 9, 1961, after collapsing near downtown's Cincinnatian Hotel. He was sixty-eight years old and had been living on the east side of Cincinnati. He is buried in the family plot at Evergreen Cemetery in Southgate, Kentucky. His obituary in the *Cincinnati Enquirer* was seven paragraphs long.

Wright, Mitchel, Thomas

The generals behind Kentucky's 'Fort' cities

Cincinnati named its first military fort for America's most famous general, George Washington. Yet, three forts that followed across the Ohio River in Kentucky bore the names Wright, Mitchell and Thomas. We all know George, but who were these other guys whose names graced the forts and ultimately became cities?

Horatio Wright (left in illustration), Ormsby Mitchel (center) and George Thomas (right) were Union generals during the Civil War. The forts named after Wright and Mitchel were built hastily in September 1862 to protect Cincinnati from Confederate Army troops that never came. The Army built Fort Thomas on high and dry ground in 1894, after Ohio and Licking river floods damaged Newport Barracks.

Horatio Wright (1820–1899)

It is unknown whether Wright, who was a top civil officer in Ohio briefly and early in the war, walked the Kenton County land that became Fort Wright. The earthen fort succumbed to development, but Wright's name stuck with incorporation of the surrounding territory as a city in 1941. His early distinctions included a sterling Army record. Years later, he engineered the completion of the Washington Monument and assisted in building the Brooklyn Bridge.

Connecticut-born Wright received an appointment to West Point at sixteen, graduating second in the Class of 1841. Wright's first Civil War assignment was to dismantle Navy ships and guns at Gosfort (later Norfolk) Navy Yard in Virginia before the Confederates could occupy it. It would be his only military failure and ended with his capture and release four days later.

Wright was at the Civil War's first major land battle known as Bull Run. During his brief service in Ohio in 1862, Wright's troops chased General Braxton Bragg out of Kentucky and helped hold the Union lines at Gettysburg. In April 1865, Wright led a charge against General Robert E. Lee during the pivotal, 292-day Siege of Petersburg. He enjoyed fifteen years of retirement before he died and was buried at Arlington National Cemetery.

Ormsby Mitchel (1810–1862)

The regional impact of Mitchel (a second "l" was added to the town for unknown reasons) came before war. The crowning achievement of the West Point-schooled attorney, surveyor, lecturer, professor and astronomer was to walk door-to-door to raise money that helped establish Cincinnati Observatory atop Mount Ida (Adams). Mitchel purchased its eleven-inch telescope in Munich, Germany. The scope still draws wows at the observatory's second location atop Mount Lookout.

Mitchel was the first director of the so-called "Lighthouse of the Sky" and published the nation's first astronomy magazine. As a soldier, Mitchel was known as "General Stars." History buffs remember him for ordering a failed raid on Confederate train robbers in Georgia that inspired Buster Keaton's 1926 iconic silent film *The General.*

Like Wright, Mitchel had a long-gone earthen fort on Dixie Highway named for him. It stuck when Fort Mitchell incorporated as a city in 1910.

The Kentucky native grew up and attended school in Lebanon, Ohio. Ironically, Mitchel's first-year roommate at the United States Military Academy was Robert E. Lee. Mitchel graduated fifteenth in the Class of 1829, worked at West Point as an assistant professor and then moved to Ohio where he became a lawyer, a renowned orator and professor at Cincinnati College, teaching math, philosophy and astronomy.

Mitchel served as chief engineer of the first Cincinnati-based railroad, the Little Miami, and plotted its line north to Springfield. While away from Cincinnati in the late 1850s, Mitchel helped establish observatories for the United States Navy and Harvard University.

Civil War broke out when Mitchel was fifty-one and working as the head astronomer at an observatory in Albany, New York. President Abraham

Lincoln appointed him brigadier general of volunteers and he orchestrated the fortification of Cincinnati against a never-realized Confederate Army invasion. Mitchel was well known for leading the Union seizure of Huntsville, Alabama, in which no shots were fired.

The Carl Sagan of his time died of yellow fever at fifty-two while serving as a major general in Beaufort, South Carolina. He was buried in Brooklyn's Green-Wood Cemetery.

George Thomas (1816–1870)

Thomas had the highest credentials of the three generals, having served a tier below Union generals Ulysses S. Grant, William Tecumseh Sherman and Philip Sheridan. Thomas was born in Virginia, gave up his Southern ties and fought with distinction in the Civil War, earning the nicknames "Rock of Chickamauga," "Sledge of Nashville" and "Pap." Due to his plodding approach to engaging the enemy, his military colleagues also referred to him as "Slow Trot Thomas." His humble demeanor deflected the spotlight that shined so bright on other generals.

Like Wright, Thomas' physical connection to his namesake fort is tenuous. Thomas, his mother and siblings fled Virginia in the wake of the 1831 Nat Turner revolt. His West Point education began in 1836, and he roomed with Sherman. His early military assignments included the Seminole War (1841–1842) and the Mexican War (1847).

Thomas taught artillery and cavalry at West Point in the early 1850s. While serving with Lee in Texas in 1860, he was hit by a Comanche arrow and took a twelve-month leave of absence. Soon after, the Civil War broke out and Thomas made a fateful decision to serve the north, effectively abandoning his family.

His rise to brigadier general was swift, and his battle duty included Chickamauga, Perryville and Mill Springs in Kentucky, Nashville and cities throughout the South that were crushed and burned by General Sherman. Post war, he commanded several military districts, including San Francisco, where he died of a stroke at age fifty-three. He was buried in Troy, New York.

XX

Henry Probasco

Tragedy haunted iconic fountain founder

Horatio Alger couldn't have written the story of Henry Probasco any better than Probasco lived it.

Born in Connecticut on the Fourth of July in 1820 to parents of unremarkable distinction, he was educated in the nation's first capital, Philadelphia. The family moved around a bit before landing in Southwest Ohio.

Probasco left home at fifteen and moved to Cincinnati, which was the American West's largest city with about 40,000 residents. He landed a job as a merchant's clerk that set in motion a roller-coaster story that included him giving the city its central landmark, Fountain Square.

Probasco was a fast learner, and in 1840 he became junior partner in Tyler Davidson & Co. Importers and Jobbers of Hardware, Cutlery and Metals. That same year at age twenty, he married Davidson's half-sister, Julia Carrington.

The force behind Probasco's storyline was his foresight and confidence. He proposed tearing down Davidson's shop and replacing it with a five-story, stone store. His brother-in-law agreed, and Davidson's became the anchor of Main Street, located approximately where Fort Washington Way is today.

Davidson's was already a major hardware store when its beautiful new building at 140–142 Main opened in 1851. Sales quadrupled in three years, making Tyler Davidson & Co. the largest hardware retailer in Cincinnati. Davidson and Probasco became wealthy.

Except for Davidson's death in 1865 and not having children, the Probascos seemingly had everything they wanted. The couple inherited most of

Davidson's riches, prompting Henry to sell the store to a partner, retire and embark on a $500,000 (more than $13 million in today's currency) project to develop a twenty-nine-acre homestead in suburban Clifton.

Probasco hired the most talented men to create what he dubbed "Oakwood." Among them were Irish architect William Tinsley, British wood carvers Henry and William Fry, New York furniture maker Herter Brothers, Italian fresco artist Francis Pedretti and German landscape architect Adolph Strauch.

The long-gone grounds—including a 4,000-plant rosarium, long driveways, stone steps, fountains, benches, lakes and trees from as far away as Japan—were of "a degree of beauty not equaled anywhere else on the American continent if in the world," wrote George M. Roe in his 1895 book *Cincinnati: The Queen City of the West.*

(The 12,047 square-foot mansion's subsequent owners have restored Oakwood's original quality, but its surrounding land was subdivided for housing decades ago.)

Henry and Julia traveled to Europe in 1867. What Probasco saw, especially in Italy and Germany, ignited his lifelong passion for literature, horticulture and the fine arts. For most of his life, Probasco collected paintings and sculpture to fill his new home. He sought out rare and centuries-old books to fill his floor-to-ceiling library that would become an important investment later in life.

He visited European foundries, too, searching for the right person to fashion a fountain fit to rival the great water features of Europe. He chose Ferdinand von Miller of the Bronze Foundry of Munich. On October 6, 1871, Probasco dedicated the fountain to his beloved brother-in-law before a crowd of 20,000. The Tyler Davidson Fountain, with its "Genius of Water" central sculpture and surrounding square have been the heart of Cincinnati ever since.

Probasco's life took a tragic turn in 1886 when Julia died of "paralysis," a nineteenth century medical term for stroke or Parkinson's disease. The sixty-seven-year-old Probasco must have been devastated and lonely—but not for long. In 1887, he married thirty-one-year-old Grace Sherlock, the daughter of one of his fellow "Seven Barons of Clifton," Thomas Sherlock. Probasco had known Grace since she was a child.

Probasco gradually sold off the bulk of his vast collections of art and books to fund this new phase of his life and retired from politics in 1888 after serving as Clifton's mayor for eleven years. Daughter Grace was born that year, and Henry Jr. followed in 1890.

Beyond the fact that he earned a little income working as president of Spring Grove Cemetery, little of Henry Probasco's life in the Gay Nineties is documented. His great-granddaughter, Whitney Rowe Long, has a few family photographs taken in the early to mid-1890s that show little Grace in a white dress accompanied by a similarly dressed doll. And there's young Henry sitting on the steps of the mansion with his mother and sister, holding a croquet mallet.

Probasco's savings apparently ran dry in 1897, however, and his creditors sued him. Court of Insolvency of Hamilton County records show Probasco was freed of his debts and received $67,000 for his Oakwood estate from Union Savings Bank and Trust in 1897. The bank then sold Oakwood to hotel founder Loretta Reakirt Gibson for $68,000, far less than the $500,000 Probasco paid to develop his estate.

By 1899, city directories showed the Probascos living on Evanswood Place in a more modest home but still in Probasco's beloved Clifton. Little Henry developed gangrene following an accident with a cap gun and died in July 1901, three days short of his eleventh birthday. A still bereaving Henry Sr. died on October 26, 1902, of pneumonia at eighty-two.

By all indications, Probasco got what he wanted out of a very full life. Exactly why his fortunes tumbled toward the end isn't clear. "Some people would say it was bad business investments," said Whitney Long's husband Phillip Long. "But for most of his life, he didn't have any children, so he gave away a lot of his money. He was a very generous man."

Henry Probasco was buried under a modest marker in a prominent lot at Spring Grove next to Julia and feet from the large pink granite monument of his brother-in-law, Tyler Davidson.

John A. Roebling

Bridge builder banked on his oldest son

There's a Roebling Street in Brooklyn, a Roebling Avenue in Los Angeles and a Roebling Museum in Roebling, New Jersey, but other than the short Roebling Road on Cincinnati's west side, the name is all about the bridge.

It was late 1866 when John A. Roebling's oldest son, Washington (right in illustration), completed the iconic Ohio River bridge that bears his father's name. Past generations knew it as the Covington-Cincinnati Bridge, the "Gateway to the South" and the "Singing Bridge," but since it was renamed in 1982, it has been the John A. Roebling Bridge.

The cable and tier technology the Roeblings developed made them the world's greatest suspension bridge builders. In New York, John's name is irrevocably tied to its Brooklyn Bridge, but in Cincinnati, people know theirs as the suspension bridge, the light blue one that hums or sings as they drive over its mesh metal deck.

Few people likely ask what kind of man made it. Roebling was highly educated, entrepreneurial and astutely successful when it came to inventing and running a business. He was a man of literature, a writer, a violinist, and a piano player, according to the Roebling Museum. He had four sons and three daughters.

But within that family, he was a relentlessly stern task master, according to Washington. In his memoir, he referred to John as either "father," "Mr. Roebling," "John A." or "Mr. R," never "Dad" or anything hinting at affection. Washington's 270-page memoir, which went unpublished for one hundred years until 2009, blames his "overbearing" father for his mother's death at forty-eight. Washington wrote that John was a "genius," who could not be challenged and claimed to know more than anyone. Wrote Washington: "In cable making he did, but not in other matters."

To those outside his family, John A. Roebling was famous and intellectual. In some ways, he also was the original Cable Guy, a sleeves-rolled-up industrialist and a problem solver. He was born Johann Augustus Roebling in 1806 in Mulhausen, Prussia (Germany), to a tobacco merchant who made sure his son received a formal education in French, drafting and mathematics. The latter two subjects and the architecture and engineering courses Roebling took at the Royal Polytechnic School in Berlin laid the foundation for his career.

In college, the science of suspension construction fascinated Roebling. After graduation, he had to put in three years of road building service, but he dreamed about suspension bridges. The Prussian state, however, denied his requests.

So a twenty-five-year-old Roebling packed up and moved with his brother, Karl, and other Germans to the United States. They settled in western Pennsylvania and founded the town of Saxonburg. In 1836, Roebling married Johanna Herting and started a family. Washington was born in 1837, the same year Johann Augustus Roebling became a United States citizen and Anglicized his name to John A. Roebling.

Roebling worked as an engineer on the Pennsylvania Canal before getting a job surveying for a railroad company in the Allegheny Mountains. The work brought the cable guy out of John Roebling. According to the Roebling Museum's biography, he loathed the limitations of hemp ropes used by canal boat captains to ascend inclines, so he invented a twisted wire rope in 1841 that became the backbone of his manufacturing business.

The John A. Roebling's Sons Co. of Trenton, New Jersey, made cables, wire and other construction products until 1953. Its products fortified the Covington-Cincinnati, Niagara, George Washington, Brooklyn and Golden Gate bridges.

A group of Covington area investors hired Roebling to design and build what at the time would be the world's longest suspension bridge (1,057 feet) to Cincinnati. Work began in 1856. An economic downturn halted construction in 1858, and the project sat dormant for several years until Civil War defense needs re-ignited interest, and investors paid to finish it.

John Roebling had been called away to New York near the war's end to design a bridge over the East River between Manhattan and Brooklyn. So he called on Washington, who had bridge-building experience as a Union officer, to complete the Covington-Cincinnati Bridge. And there was a lot left to be done.

Hailed by the *Cincinnati Enquirer* as "the greatest work in the country," the suspension bridge opened to 40,000 pedestrians on Saturday, December 1, 1866. On Sunday, another 120,000 walked the world-class bridge linking the North and the South.

The bridge opened to vehicles on January 1, 1867, a day when the river was so icy it could not be navigated by the ferry operators, who had fervently opposed the bridge, fearing that it would put them out of business. A huge crowd lined a parade route from downtown to the bridge. In the line were eight-horse cargo wagons, community bands and bridge company and city dignitaries.

Was John A. Roebling there at the christening? It's possible, but his name was not in the *Cincinnati Enquirer's* opening day article. It could have been that Roebling, now chief engineer of the New York Bridge Co., was in New York, where he would die before seeing Washington build the Brooklyn Bridge, a two-tier, double-wide version of the Covington-Cincinnati Bridge.

Roebling was surveying a centerline for the New York bridge on a Fulton Ferry slip in July 1869 when a boat crashed and crushed his foot. At first, Roebling eschewed medical advice. Then, some of his toes were amputated, and he developed tetanus. Sixteen days after the accident, the infection killed John A. Roebling.

Washington Roebling—debilitated by a case of the "bends" (decompression sickness) that he contracted while working in pressurized underwater chambers during bridge construction—took over the project. On most days, he was too sick to go outside, so he watched progress through a nearby apartment window as his wife, Emily Warren Roebling, orchestrated the completion of the iconic bridge in 1883.

That same year, *Harper's Weekly* honored John A. Roebling with a large political cartoon that showed him climbing down the end of the bridge. Under the image was the caption: "New York Entrance to the Brooklyn Bridge. Evidence the elevated gentleman intends to stay."

Nellie Taft

Determined dreamer created her own high life

Bright, progressive and blessed to be part of Cincinnati's most powerful political family, Helen "Nellie" Louise Herron (born in 1861) formed her life's ambition at age sixteen: She would marry a powerful man, he would become president of the United States, and she would live in the White House.

The man she married in 1886, Cincinnati lawyer and judge William Howard Taft, had his own ambition: He wanted to be Chief Justice of the United States Supreme Court.

Both ambitions were realized, but who got theirs first? Nellie Taft—by twelve years, the same number of years by which she outlived her husband. Nellie's exciting, dream-like life ended in 1943, and she became the first woman to be buried at Arlington National Cemetery.

Nellie's life highlights appear to paint her as a successful and stand-up, turn-of-the-century woman. They include her seminal role in the Cincinnati Symphony Orchestra's early years, her rearing of three children (including Robert A., three-term U.S. senator and three-time presidential candidate; and Helen, president of Bryn Mawr College), her ascension to the White House, and her long, loyal marriage to a brilliant man.

But lesser-known tidbits about Nellie Herron Taft add spice to her story. According to the National First Ladies' Library, Nellie Taft enjoyed racy theater productions, played poker for money, smoked cigarettes and drank alcohol, sometimes on Sundays. She brought champagne punch back into the White House while temperance supporters were pushing for Prohibition.

Those beautiful cherry trees that blossom each spring in the Potomac River Tidal Basin in Washington are among her lasting achievements, as she lobbied Congress aggressively to contribute $25,000 (more than $620,000 in today's currency) to buy and plant the heralded trees.

Nellie was educated in four foreign languages in Cincinnati. When her husband served as the governor-general of the Philippines from 1900 to 1903, Nellie learned to speak the native Tagalog language and accepted invitations to Filipinos' special events. She embraced the culture and people like no other Anglo-Saxon woman before her, according to the Ladies' Library.

When Nellie's judicially minded husband hesitated to leave the Philippines to become President Theodore Roosevelt's War Secretary, she urged him on until he accepted the appointment. But Nellie, the library wrote, found being a Cabinet member's wife "dull and demeaning." She wanted to be more than a visitor in the White House. She wanted it to be her home so badly she lobbied Roosevelt privately—and successfully—to help get "Big Bill" onto the Republican ticket in 1908.

Nellie might not have trusted Roosevelt, who many thought would renege on his promise to eschew a second term and make a run at the nomination at the 1908 GOP convention. She went all out, albeit privately, to guide William Howard Taft to victory.

Here is the Ladies' Library's account: "In dozens of letters, she advised him on how to position himself, sometimes down to what words to use, so that he would be seen as supporting some of Roosevelt's popular policies yet also standing on his own, apart from Roosevelt."

The Tafts were making a rare visit to the Cincinnati home of William's older brother Charles Phelps Taft (now the Taft Museum of Art), when they received the official confirmation of William's presidential nomination. An ecstatic crowd smothered Fountain Square and the Taft house where Taft delivered his acceptance speech from its portico.

Nellie appeared once with her husband during his campaign, but on Inauguration Day March 4, 1909, she was the first first lady to parade to the White House seated next to the new president—and the first to do so in an automobile.

Nellie's progressive ways continued in the White House. She hired African Americans as ushers, positions historically reserved for whites. She lifted the ban against divorced visitors, hosted concerts and opened the White House grounds to the public for special events in a way no first lady ever had.

Initially, Nellie was a political force as well. She was the impetus behind an executive order that required the Bureau of Public Health to improve the working conditions of women in the executive branch of the federal government. That and other efforts inspired some historians to describe her as a civil rights activist.

Much of Nellie's political activity eventually leaked through the press, but mostly she stayed out of the public eye, especially after she had a serious stroke in May 1909. Her convalescence was long, as she had to learn to speak, read and write again. She came out of it with a slightly droopy face, a limited vocabulary and a permanent speech impediment.

Wrote presidential historian Feather Schwartz Foster: "In short, while the 'receptor' part of her brain, the part that could understand everything, was intact, the 'transmitter' part, the part that could communicate, was seriously impaired. It would take the rest of Taft's administration for her to regain the better part of her lost abilities."

Nellie kept a low public profile for other reasons, according to the Ladies' Library: "Although there is not even circumstantial suggestion that she was ever an alcoholic, she was a heavy drinker, with a self-proclaimed taste for quality beer and champagne."

In the waning months of Bill's presidency, Nellie emerged from her seclusion in a big way when she attended the 1912 Democratic National Convention. She was the first and last first lady to attend an opposing party's convention. She broke ranks again after her husband was confirmed as Chief Justice in 1921, supporting the League of Nations and opposing Prohibition.

Her crossing the aisle continued in the twelve years she lived after her husband died in 1931, becoming friends with Eleanor Roosevelt and reportedly supporting the 1936 re-election campaign of Franklin Roosevelt, who hired her son, Robert A. Taft Sr., to work for the New Deal.

Clement Barnhorn

Under-radar sculptor was his generation's best

A third-floor studio in the original Art Academy of Cincinnati building in Eden Park was named for sculpture department head Clement John Barnhorn, and the story goes that he kept a yellow canary up there to keep him company. Legend also has it that school staff members sometimes whistled up the stairwell in hopes that Barnhorn's bird would reply to them in song.

The canary story is the most unexpected nugget contained in the Cincinnati Art Museum library's file on Barnhorn. Pieced together, however, its twenty-five-pages weave a story that shows why Barnhorn was arguably the most important Cincinnati sculptor of his generation, much like Hiram Powers was before him. The great sculptor, however, worked in the shadow of his friend and school studio partner, painter Frank Duveneck. Obscurity was Barnhorn's destiny.

Written homages to Barnhorn—whose architectural sculpture, Rookwood Pottery fountains, memorials and ecclesiastic and funerary works can be found throughout the Cincinnati region—describe him as meek, modest, gentile, generous, publicity shy and deeply religious. He attended Mass, often with Duveneck, and never married.

The 1910 Census shows that Barnhorn, at the age of fifty-seven, was a lodger at 318 Broadway, downtown. He had a studio in the six-story Pike Building on Fourth Street, according to Cynthia Mills' 2014 book *Beyond Grief: Sculpture and Wonder in the Gilded Age Cemetery.*

Cincinnati sculptor Ernest Bruce Haswell (1899–1965) studied under Barnhorn at the Art Academy and likely spent hours with him, at and away from school. Wrote Haswell: "Barnhorn's means were barely enough for the necessities of life. He practiced pitiful economies, banished indulgences and worked with undimmed ambition, as many artists had done before."

It was in Barnhorn's downtown studio where Duveneck sculpted a funerary monument of his deceased wife, Elizabeth "Lizzie" Boott. Duveneck's first sculpture was completed under Barnhorn's tutelage and with his tools. Duveneck, who like Barnhorn was of German heritage and taught at the Art Academy, always acknowledged his friend's role in creating Lizzie's effigy, the plaster model of which is displayed in the Cincinnati Wing at Cincinnati Art Museum.

Barnhorn was born to German parents in Cincinnati in 1857. His father, Clemens, was a downtown tavern keeper and wholesale liquor dealer. Clement had four brothers, Henry being his twin. The Barnhorn twins lived together until Henry's death in 1907.

An average-sized man, Barnhorn attended St. Xavier College in downtown Cincinnati and then the McMicken School of Design and Drawing (renamed the Art Academy of Cincinnati in 1879). For eleven years, he studied marble carving under Italian Louis T. Rebisso—whom Barnhorn would succeed in 1899 as the academy's sculpture department head—and wood carving under the great Englishman Henry L. Fry.

After Barnhorn opened a downtown studio in 1888 and finished his apprenticeships, the school paid for him to study for five years in Paris plus six months in Italy. Barnhorn headed the Cincinnati Art Club and started his teaching at the Art Academy upon his return to his hometown.

His experience abroad, which Barnhorn reinforced with several other visits to Europe, formed his classic style and taught him to sculpt in wood, marble, bronze, clay, plaster, ceramics and stone. The *Cincinnati Enquirer* wrote: "The work that Mr. Barnhorn has been doing is like looking backwards into the middle ages, when a sculptor with slaves, who were artists, and stone cutters, worked in some cases a lifetime, to enrich and beautify the Cathedrals of Europe."

The sculptor exhibited in Europe and the United States, winning many honors. The 1895 Paris Salon awarded him an honorable mention for his sculpture "Magdalen," and the 1900 Paris Exposition gave him a bronze for his bas-relief "Madonna." The Pan-American Exposition in Buffalo (1901) and the Louisiana Purchase Exposition in St. Louis (1904 World's Fair) awarded Barnhorn medals, as well.

His largest local exhibit occurred at the Cincinnati Art Museum in 1914. It featured sixty-two photos and examples of his sculpture, including an altar relief of "Madonna" for Rookwood founder Maria Longworth Storer, a Baldwin piano, a bronze portrait of Duveneck and the often-copied sculpture "Boy with Dolphin."

Several regional cemeteries feature Barnhorn bronzes. At the center of Covington's Mother of God Cemetery is Barnhorn's four-person crucifixion scene, and four angels spread their wings to guard the corners of Duveneck's pink granite monument. Barnhorn also sculpted the six life-size bronze statues of military men and a pioneer that stand on the upper façade of Memorial Hall on Elm Street, in Over-the-Rhine.

Other accessible Barnhorn works include six pieces in the art museum's Cincinnati Wing, including "Fountain of the Water Nymph," the William Henry Harrison statue (assistant to Rebisso) in Piatt Park; the tympanum arch in limestone over the central doors at St. Mary's Basilica, Covington; the bas-relief in bronze on the Frederick W. Galbraith memorial bench near Twin Lakes, Eden Park; "Grief" on the grave marker of Cincinnati furrier A. E. Burkhardt and the Battle of Chickamauga scene on General William H. Lytle's monument, both at Spring Grove Cemetery.

Perhaps Barnhorn's most unusual creations no longer exist: large side panels sculpted in bronze for a 1929 Sayers and Scovill hearse that depicted the Angel of Memory. Barnhorn signed each panel. The appropriately named Signed Sculpture hearse was priced at $8,500 (more than $135,000 today). The Great Depression limited production to a few hearses and ended Barnhorn's foray into the automotive world.

Barnhorn died at seventy-eight in August 1935. His monument at St. Mary Cemetery in St. Bernard features his bronze sculpture of Christ on the cross. Archbishop John T. McNicholas delivered the eulogy at a requiem Mass for Barnhorn in St. Xavier Church. Said the archbishop of Barnhorn: "He knew well the teachings of his holy religion and exemplified them by his beautiful life."

XXIV

Julius Dexter

Quiet force was 'Mr. Cincinnati' of his time

The news shocked Cincinnatians. Julius Dexter, wealthy businessman, former state senator, recent candidate for governor, humble philanthropist and devoted civil servant, died suddenly on Sunday, October 21, 1898. His big heart had given out. Dexter was fifty-eight.

Flags flew at half staff over City Hall and at his beloved Queen City Club. The city scrambled to replace the man who had handled its finances for the past decade, and hundreds of people in the numerous clubs and organizations he helped form and administer around the city mourned.

Two days later, Dexter's funeral was held at Christ Episcopal Church down the street from his home, the 1840s Dexter mansion at Fourth Street and Broadway. The praise for Dexter—a single man who steadfastly opposed the corrupt political regime of George "Boss" Cox and secretly passed on his salary to needy causes in his final twenty years—gushed from the citizenry.

An October 23, 1898, *Cincinnati Enquirer* obituary read: "Few men could be taken from life who could leave behind them more vacancies in position and regard among their fellow men than does Mr. Dexter."

Despite all the admiration, little of Dexter's mark on Cincinnati is visible today. A handsome reception hall on the third floor of Music Hall, whose 1878 building committee he had chaired, bore his name until 1973 when it was renamed after the late philanthropist J. Ralph Corbett. Two streets in East Walnut Hills bear the Dexter name, probably because Julius' older brother, Charles, was an early developer of that then-rural suburb. Charles' house still stands on Dexter Place, which spans Madison Road and Dexter Avenue.

So no, you won't find the name Julius Dexter around town. Yet one of his accomplishments, the striking, gothic-inspired Dexter Mausoleum at Spring Grove Cemetery, is seen by dozens of admirers every week.

Its rare flying buttress design was created by architect James Keys Wilson, who ran in Dexter's powerful circle of families that included Longworth, Goshorn, Pendleton, Nichols, Erkenbrecher, Sinton, Springer and Hannaford. Dexter Mausoleum was built to honor the life of his father, British immigrant Edmund Dexter, a wealthy downtown liquor wholesaler and booze blender, who instilled the importance of education and public service in Julius.

Edmund died at age sixty-one in 1862 in New York after a trip abroad. The family patriarch, who also had his hand in banking and insurance interests, served the Cincinnati Literary Club, First Unitarian Church and many cultural organizations. Julius, by this time, had a bachelor's degree from Harvard and would earn a law degree from Cincinnati College a few years later. He and his four brothers—Charles, Edmund Jr., George and Adolphus—acquired what historians have described as a "liberal," "adequate" and "comfortable" inheritance. Each probably inherited a small fortune.

Charles, a poet and Harvard University graduate, took his money and became a country gentleman-father. Edmund continued to run the family business downtown. George became a well-known attorney in Boston, and Adolphus attended the U.S. Naval Academy in Annapolis, Maryland, advancing to lieutenant.

Which of the brothers funded the design and construction of Dexter Mausoleum isn't known, but given that Charles, Edmund and Julius stayed in Cincinnati, it could be that they worked as a team. The mausoleum cost $100,000 in 1866, more than $1.5 million in today's currency. Unfortunately, its stained-glass features and elevator were never completed and a storm likely felled its steeple.

Lore has it that the brothers ran out of money. Probably not, said Phil Nuxhall, author of two books about the cemetery and its former historian. "It could be there was a family quarrel, or during construction one of the workers might have died. That could have stopped it. It's another one of those mysteries here."

Julius Dexter was born to Edmund and Mary Ann Dexter on September 23, 1840. He attended Brooks Classical School, then Harvard and Cincinnati College. His 1871 passport application describes him as having light brown hair and blue eyes. He stood five-feet ten-and-a-half-inches tall. In an era where many men sported full beards, a bespectacled Dexter sports a neatly trimmed mustache or is clean shaven in photos on file at the Cincinnati Historical Library and Archives.

Julius worked alongside brothers Charles and Edmund in the liquor business until he earned his law degree. He practiced law but ultimately decided to pursue his passion for business and community service. Over the remaining three decades of his life, Dexter was a leader and financial contributor to many important institutions, including the Queen City Club, Commercial Club of Cincinnati and other institutions that advocated music, historical, technical, business, zoological, archaeological and astronomical education.

Dexter was president of the Cincinnati, Hamilton & Dayton Railroad, president and director of the Fidelity Safe Deposit & Trust Co., and a director of the Washington Fire & Marine Insurance Co. He served as a Republican in the Ohio State Senate from 1862 to 1864. Twenty years later, after reading the results of an important political poll, Dexter switched to the Democratic Party. He ran as a Gold Democrat in what he knew was a hopeless campaign for governor in the last year of his life.

Dexter made what perhaps was his greatest civic impact as a trustee of Cincinnati's Sinking Fund. He led the board for more than a decade during the corrupt Boss Cox era, administering the city's finances, including investments and debt. In a tribute book by Dexter's thirty-year housemate and companion, Eugene Bliss, Unitarian Reverend George A. Thayer is quoted as saying that Julius was "the guardian of fiscal integrity" and "a beacon of independence, courage and disinterested patriotism."

Think about that if you visit the Dexter Mausoleum at Spring Grove Cemetery. Tour guides describe it as a monument to a whiskey baron. Yet about twenty Dexters rest there, and the most impactful on Queen City history was the baron's number four son, Julius.

ELIZABETH NOURSE

'The first woman painter of America'

You won't see Elizabeth Nourse's name on a Cincinnati building or street sign. Nope. The fine artist, once considered America's best female painter, has a much bigger presence. Walk along Cincinnati's East Eighth Street between Walnut and Main and look to the south. There she is, forty-feet-high on the back of an old brick building.

It's a wonderful reproduction of her 1892 self portrait, yet it stands with no title and no explanation of the fact that Nourse painted it using a mirror, so the resulting reflection shows her painting left-handed when, in fact, she was a righty.

Nourse's local legacy isn't a secret, but it pales in comparison with her male colleagues. Perhaps that's partly because she spent most of her painting days overseas or that, despite being one of ten siblings, she never had any children of her own to perpetuate her story. Perhaps it's because she was a proper Victorian woman, a quiet Catholic who didn't get rich or toot her own horn.

Born in 1859, Elizabeth Nourse was a very big deal in the art world during the Gilded Age, so big she was dubbed "the first woman painter of America" by the *Chicago Tribune*. Nourse and her twin sister, Adelaide, were born north of Cincinnati in Mount Healthy to banker Caleb Nourse and his wife, Elizabeth Rogers Nourse. The twins and their older sister, Louise, watched their father's business fail during the Civil War. This likely taught the Nourse women a sense of independence, according to Nourse authority, Mary Alice Heekin Burke.

The Cincinnati Art Museum docent wrote that Nourse showed artistic talent as a girl, and, at age fifteen in 1874, she enrolled in the city's top art school, the McMicken School of Design, later the Art Academy of Cincinnati. Because of her residency—the family had moved into Cincinnati—she paid no tuition and was in the first life drawing classes offered to women.

The death of their parents in 1880 strengthened the bond between Elizabeth and Louise, and they became companions in life, and partners in business. Following her graduation in 1881, McMicken offered Nourse a teaching job, but she declined, believing she could make a living as a fine artist.

The mecca for painters in the 1880s was Paris, and Elizabeth aspired to study there. She attended art school briefly in New York but returned to Cincinnati for six years, saving money for her ticket to Paris. Nourse painted portraits and flowers in oil and drew important Cincinnati residences in pen and ink. She also illustrated for magazines and decorated murals. "She did anything she had to do to make a living," said Julie Aronson, a long-time curator of American Paintings, Sculpture and Drawings at the Cincinnati Art Museum.

Elizabeth, along with Louise, who was her housekeeper, secretary and business manager, embarked for Paris in August 1887. Elizabeth was twenty-eight when she enrolled at Academie Julian. All she knew were the Midwestern subjects she painted with techniques she learned at McMicken and on her own. It was plenty. The school said she was ready to turn professional after three months.

But the cards were stacked against women painters during the Victorian Era (1837–1901), especially this unknown talent from Cincinnati. Parisian cafes, where painters gathered to talk shop, were off limits to women, and art exhibitions (salons), where newcomers could launch their careers, were juried by men.

Her major subject matter—common folk, many of them women at work —was not mainstream, and her painting style was more realistic than impressionistic, which was the rage at the time. Wrote Burke: "She was a Victorian lady with all the virtues we associate with them—she was religious, devoted to her family, patriotic and hard working. Yet she was also independent, courageous and determined to make a successful career in a field where many men failed to make a living."

It took Nourse seven years and five exhibitions to sell for $300 what would become one of her most famous paintings, "La Mere," a simple portrait of a mother holding her child on her lap. That painting eventually hung in President Woodrow Wilson's Princeton, New Jersey, studio.

The signature on "La Mere" read "E. Nourse," probably so that no one would know it had been painted by a woman. She changed her signature to Elizabeth Nourse in 1904 and never looked back. During the peak years of her career, she traveled throughout Europe, Russia and North Africa, always accompanied by Louise.

In each country, she studied the costumes and culture, the quality of sunlight and the overall environment. "She had a deep respect for learning as well for the nuns she befriended and stayed with on her travels," Aronson said.

Her paintings found homes on the walls of famous European galleries along with those by John Singer Sargent, James Abbot McNeill Whistler and Winslow Homer. Nourse became the second American woman elected to the Societe National des Beaux-Arts, a union of important art exhibitions. Later, she became its first female president. She won awards at exhibitions overseas and across the United States, proving she was no "Sunday painter."

But everything changed for Nourse with world war in 1914. She and Louise stayed in France. They traveled to Brittany to help war widows. "It is quite a sight to see us bringing in the cows and tossing the hay, feeding ducks, chickens and picking beets and cabbage leaves for cattle," Elizabeth wrote to a friend.

Nourse returned to painting after the war. She underwent surgery for breast cancer in 1920 but, once again, persevered. Art critics, however, had new tastes, and Nourse stopped exhibiting in 1924, painting only for pleasure after that.

Louise died in 1937. Elizabeth died on October 8, 1938, at age seventy-eight and was buried next to Louise in Saint Leger, southwest of Paris. Several of Nourse's paintings hang in the Cincinnati Wing of the Cincinnati Art Museum in Eden Park.

Stephen Gerrard

Sales innovator earned the title 'Cantaloupe King'

Like Cincinnati grocery magnate Bernard "Barney" Kroger, Stephen Anderson Gerrard (1860–1936) went from being a produce peddler in downtown Cincinnati to living in an upscale suburban neighborhood. His impact on the development, transportation and sale of produce was so great that he became known as the "Cantaloupe King."

Some people recognize that moniker. Few know the name Stephen Gerrard. Likely, those who do either have toured his Tudor revival mansion in North Avondale or been inside his Spring Grove Cemetery mausoleum that Gerrard's descendants occasionally open for viewing.

That pearly white, art deco-style mausoleum stands on a prominent intersection just beyond the cemetery's railroad bridge and is testimony that Stephen Gerrard, though nearly broken by the Great Depression, was most worthy of an impressive final resting place. Granted, the Gerrard name can't compete with Kroger, William Procter or James Gamble, but his life story can.

Gerrard was born on a farm east of Cincinnati in Cherry Grove, a small village that is now just inside the I-275 beltway. He was the fifth of eight children. According to *Memoirs of the Miami Valley, Vol. 3* by John Hover and Joseph Barnes (1920), Gerrard attended school there, likely with his future wife, Estella Markley, whose family owned large parcels of farmland in southeastern Hamilton County known as Five Mile.

After marrying on December 29, 1880, Gerrard worked for three years on fourteen acres in the "truck and berries" business. Every July through Thanksgiving, he worked the dirt streets of Cincinnati—by then a bustling metropolis of 255,000 people—rising at 2 a.m. to buy the freshest produce he could and then peddling it from a cart.

Hover and Barnes wrote that Gerrard slept on a bed of hay in a stable, using "the good mosquitoes for my alarm clock in the morning." Gerrard would return home by 6 p.m. Saturday and spend Sunday with his wife and their son, Virgil.

The family moved downtown into a two-room residence on Third Street in 1883. Gerrard hauled coal for $2 a day in the winter and saved $400 that first year. Three years of sweat bought him four new produce wagons and a partnership with Estella's cousin, Hiram Markley.

The duo sold carloads of produce in the Cincinnati, Hamilton and Dayton rail yards and launched Markley & Gerrard at 236 W. Sixth St. in 1885. Their business thrived for ten years. The Gerrards had a daughter and another son, who died as an infant.

It was in the ten years after poor health forced Markley to leave the business and move to Arizona that Gerrad struck it rich. He traveled out West and fell in love with cantaloupes in California. He longed to introduce them to Cincinnati, but the fruit was too delicate to survive the long train ride home.

The plucky Gerrard, however, came up with a solution. He developed the first refrigerated railcar. By 1905, he stabled 134 of the cold cars in Colorado and began transporting fresh cantaloupes to the Midwest and eventually to California, Arizona and New Mexico.

Stephen and Estella had moved around the city to neighborhoods such as Mount Auburn and Price Hill after their surviving son and daughter moved out, but in 1915 they built a new Gothic-Tudor revival mansion on Betula Avenue in a high-end subdivision of North Avondale. The house stands near the northern boundary of Cincinnati's corporation limit on land once owned by furniture magnate Robert Mitchell.

The seven-gabled Gerrard House is in the well-known Rose Hill subdivision near Reading Road and Clinton Springs Avenue. The house has been well-preserved over its one hundred-plus years and was added to the National Register of Historic Places in 1987. It has exterior electric outlets for Christmas lights that were unheard of at the time. The interior boasts teakwood floors, Italian marble columns, wall murals and a cavernous music room built especially for Estella that features, what was in its day, the largest residential pipe organ in the country.

The house's Kimball organ, which could play by itself, places it in the company of other well-known Cincinnati mansions with similar instruments, such as River High in Hyde Park, the Stearns Mansion in Wyoming and Bishop's Place in Clifton. It was said to be wired like a 1915 computer and too expensive to restore once it stopped working.

Gerrard incorporated the S.A. Gerrard and Co. in 1921. That year, he moved 2,719 railcars of cantaloupes and employed 123 sales agents, according to Hover and Barnes. Gerrard popularized iceberg lettuce and began hybridizing melons, among them the Honey Dew and Elberta Peach, which he named after his daughter. Other melon varieties he sold were Pink Queen, American Beauty and Beekman Breakfast.

Gerrard, who was a Baptist and a 32nd degree Mason, had faced and survived court battles throughout his successful years, but shortly after he took his company public, the stock market crashed. Gerrard crashed with it when he tried to buy back the stock. Legend has it that he used most of what was left of his fortune, $125,000 (about $2 million in today's currency), on his mausoleum, construction of which began in 1930, six years before his death.

The mausoleum is a blend of neo-classical and art deco architecture with Arts & Crafts touches. It features four allegorical marble statues inside that represent the seasons and lion-head gargoyles placed at the peak of its roof to ward off evil spirits. To see it, enter the main gates of Spring Grove Cemetery, drive straight and under the railroad bridge and take the first right. It stands at the first V in the road, the first of several mausoleums of famous Cincinnatians on the cemetery's Cedar and Sylvan lakes.

The cemetery's death card for Gerrard shows that the "Cantaloupe King" died seven days short of his seventy-sixth birthday on February 16, 1936, of "paralytic stroke, cerebral hemorrhage and arteriosclerosis."

John Uri Lloyd

Oldest brother imprinted science, science fiction

They were three rambunctious boys who played in the wild woods of Boone County, Kentucky, yet when they emerged as men across the Ohio River in Cincinnati, they became generous leaders in pharmaceutical research and development, professional baseball and, of all things, the study of mushrooms.

The sons of Marvin and Sophia, two upstate New York teachers, were John Uri, Nelson Ashley and Curtis Gates Lloyd. They might not be on every Cincinnati historian's A-list, but the trio left a legacy of the unique Lloyd Library and Museum in downtown Cincinnati.

The Lloyd Library, which today is free and open to the public, was established by John in the 1870s. Over the years, it provided nature-based drug research for the Lloyd brothers, students and scholars. The library incorporated as part of a trust established by Curtis in 1917. It was built on the foundation of John's personal library that had grown to thousands of scientific volumes, the majority of them amassed by John and Curtis.

The middle son, Ashley (1851–1926), quietly built a career in pharmaceuticals and baseball. He managed the brothers' books, co-owned the Cincinnati Reds and spearheaded the construction of the first concrete baseball park, Cincinnati's Palace of the Fans. He was part-owner and treasurer of the New York Giants.

The flashier Curtis (1858–1926) traveled the world, photographing plants and their uses and gathering specimens and rare books now in the Lloyd Library. But his passion was collecting and identifying mushroom strains around the world. At one point, the international fungi authority's herbarium housed 60,000 specimens.

Meanwhile, John (1849–1936) hunkered down in Cincinnati and became an eclectic medicine pioneer, plant-medicine and laboratory equipment inventor, professor and science fiction writer. As one of the world's top pharmacists and herbalists, he achieved a higher profile than his brothers and helped transition the use of medicinal plants from quackery to science. He is credited with changing the role of the pharmacist from medicine maker to medicine dispenser, which drew the ire of his colleagues who exiled him to the back pages of recorded history.

Nevertheless, Lloyd was influential as a scholar, inventor, businessman, teacher and author of fiction, including books about his beloved Boone County. He is remembered for his invention of the "cold still" for plant extractions as well as the buffered alkaloid called alcresta.

Then there was his 1895 underworld adventure novel *Etidorhpa, or the End of the Earth.* Lloyd spelled Aphrodite backward for its title and imagined the Earth was hollow, as did Jules Verne in *Journey to the Center of the Earth.* His protagonist enters through a cave in Kentucky and has physical transcendental experiences, among others, on his way to the Earth's core. It is a one-of-a-kind novel in literature and became a cult classic among non-traditional thinkers in the United States and Europe.

John was born in upstate New York in 1849. Two years after his brother Ashley was born in 1851, the family moved to Boone County, settling first in Petersburg and then Florence, where John witnessed a Civil War skirmish.

John wrote later in life that while playing in the Northern Kentucky woods, he dreamed of becoming a trapper like Daniel Boone. But his keener interest was in science, and although he was too young to study chemistry in school, he conducted his own experiments in his backyard laboratory. His family noticed John's advanced work with plants and chemistry and took him to Cincinnati where he could work with a mentor.

John's first apprenticeship in pharmacy came at age fourteen with W.J.M. Gordon in his office at Ninth and Central Avenue, future site of City Hall. Gordon was the only person west of the Allegheny Mountains making glycerin, and he taught John pharmaceutical principles as well as how a product that was made cheaply, simply and rapidly could make a lot of money.

A second, two-year apprenticeship followed with Cincinnati's European trained pharmacist George Eger, whose expertise was using plants in medicine. John learned how to incorporate poppy-based opium, hemp, valerian root, mayapple, goldenseal, black hellebore, belladonna and many other botanicals into his eclectic medicine research and development.

John was just twenty-one in 1870 when he found himself working within the core of Cincinnati's medical community. He befriended and impressed eclectic physician John King, who helped him become a chemist, launching Lloyd's lifelong career in pharmacy.

John's first wife, Cincinnati teacher Addie Meader, died in 1877 at age twenty-one just eleven days after they married. He and his second wife, Boone County native Emma Rouse, married in 1880. They bought the stone mansion built by James W. McLaughlin at the top of then-suburban Clifton Avenue's northern hill. The Lloyds had two daughters and one son.

The 1880s were a busy time for the energetic John. He was a professor of chemistry at the Eclectic Medical Institute (1878–1895) and the Cincinnati College of Pharmacy (1883–1887). In 1886, he, Ashley and Curtis founded Lloyd Brothers Pharmacists.

John was a highly respected yet somewhat odd instructor who would not let his pupils take notes. One student described him entering the classroom this way: "Small of stature and spare of form; neat as a new pin; unostentatious to an extreme; dressed very plainly but faultlessly, and always with a small nosegay, preferably a delicate little rose in the button hole of the left lapel of his coat; noiselessly he entered, and with a quick, quiet, elastic step reached the platform..."

Awards and commendations showered down on John over the years, and his reputation spread nationally and internationally. He and his brothers were known to donate medicine to needy Americans, and John contributed to the creation and enactment of the Pure Food and Drug Act of 1906.

John Uri Lloyd lived most his last fifty-six years in Clifton, dying ten days before his eighty-seventh birthday while visiting his daughter, Annie, in Los Angeles. He is buried in Hopeful Lutheran Church Cemetery in Florence, Kentucky.

Charlie Grant

Second baseman first among 'almost famous'

Charlie Grant was one train ride away from becoming the first African American to play major league baseball. Had Baltimore Orioles manager and future Hall-of-Famer John McGraw gotten away with his scheme to pass the light-skinned Grant off as the American Indian "Tokohama" in 1901, perhaps Jackie Robinson would have gone down as the second Black player in "the bigs."

To be truthful, Grant was no Jackie Robinson. They both played second base and were slick fielders and fast runners, but Grant, whose nicknames were "Speedy" and "Cincy," didn't have Robinson's bat or dashing good looks. Nevertheless, his story—though mostly forgotten—is a crazy one.

First, there's the fuzziness of his exact date of birth in Cincinnati to Charles Grant Jr. and Mary Grant. The 1880 census lists it as 1876. Grant's draft registration papers say 1877. His marker at Cincinnati's Spring Grove Cemetery—which features balls and two crossed baseball bats—says he was born in 1874.

The family lived their early days several miles north of downtown near the cemetery. Grant's father was a hostler, a defunct term for a horse groomsman or stableman. Charlie learned to play baseball in the Queen City and would end his career playing for the Cincinnati Stars.

The right-hander grew to be five-feet-eight-inches tall and weighed a solid 175 pounds. It was said that he had been a pitcher and invented the baffling screwball before he settled in as a second baseman.

Grant started his career in 1896 with the Page Fence Giants of Adrian, Michigan, one of the first professional barnstorming Black teams. How they got around the Midwest was part of their appeal and success, according to Brian McKenna, a biographer for the Society of American Baseball Research.

McKenna wrote that, according to the Negro League Baseball Players Association, the Michigan team "traveled around the country in a custom-made railroad car, which featured sleeping quarters, a cook and a porter." The players drummed up pre-game enthusiasm for the Giants by riding bicycles around towns while dressed in full uniform.

A little more than ten years into his two-decade career, Grant married Cincinnati telephone operator Eva May Irvin, but they divorced sometime between 1911 and 1918. After winning several championships in the days before the first Negro league formed, Grant retired in 1916 and returned to Cincinnati to live with his parents.

Both he and his father, census records show, worked as apartment complex janitors, and it was in front of the Gilbert Avenue building in which Charlie lived on July 9, 1932, that a car struck and killed him. Wrote McKenna: "Charles Grant was sitting and relaxing on the sidewalk outside his apartment when a passing motorist, whose tire blew, jumped the curb and slammed into the ex-ballplayer."

Thirty-one years before that, Grant nearly made his improbable breakthrough into the major leagues. Grant caught the eye of John McGraw, one of the biggest-named managers in the brand new American League. In those days, there was a lot of "tampering and contract jumping," McKenna wrote, and managers like McGraw pulled out all the stops to put together the best team possible.

The resorts in Hot Springs, Arkansas, were a big off-season draw for white players and managers. Many African-American players worked in the town's hotels and bathhouses. Grant was a bell hop there in the Eastman Hotel and part of a player tryout held on the hotel's lawn in early March 1901.

The Black players, Grant among them, organized their own games and drew the watchful eye of ruthless recruiters like McGraw. Grant, with his light skin, straight hair and high cheekbones as well as his excellent fielding and base-running skills, impressed McGraw.

The story gets murky after that. One journalist claimed he had convinced the trusted manager to pass Grant off as an Indian who, unlike Blacks, could play in the majors. McGraw began touting his new find as Charlie Tokohama, a supposed Cherokee named after a creek McGraw reportedly saw on a map in the Eastman Hotel lobby. The problem is, there is no such creek. Possibly another glitch in the scheme was that Grant and several of his teammates reportedly didn't buy into the scam.

Still, the scheme of McGraw and the journalist gained momentum—possibly too much—during spring training. Baseball writers and the staff of Chicago White Sox owner Charles Comiskey who had seen Grant play for Black teams in Chicago, were dubious and shared their concerns in newspaper columns in the Midwest and East.

Several Oriole players, Grant among them, were due to board a train from Hot Springs to Baltimore on March 29, 1901. But the press revealed McGraw's ruse, and "Tokohama" never got on that train. Instead, he boarded one to Chicago, where he began to play as Charlie Grant again, this time for the all-Black Union Giants on April 6. Perhaps Grant felt relieved, although research could not confirm that he was.

The Windy City, embraced "Our boy, Charlie Grant" upon his return, McKenna wrote, but the second baseman defected to Philadelphia. Grant played out his career with two other teams before retiring from the Cincinnati Stars in 1916 at age forty-two. Or was he forty? Possibly thirty-nine? His age was never an issue in his career, but fans' fascination with his stint as "Tokohama" was.

Wrote McKenna: "This is an early instance in which men of darker skin had to pass themselves off as someone acceptable to white baseball executives and fans. In the case of Grant, that was as a Native American....The stunt came to define Grant's career. From 1901 through the end of his career, he was a major attraction because of it."

More of a major attraction was the Negro National League, created by Rube Foster four years after Grant retired. Charlie missed by that much his best chance to play in "the bigs."

Franklin Enger

Automaker had a 'what-could-have-been' life

Frank Enger's breakout year as an automobile maker should have been 1916. In his seventh year as president of Enger Motor Car Co., the first-generation German-American had just released his fifth model since 1909, the year he transformed the family's buggy business into a horseless carriage company.

Enger Motor Car had reorganized and joined the stock market in 1916, with Frank being the majority holder of $1.2 million of the $4 million in stock. Enger's new Twin Six, a 12-cylinder touring model with a lever that could switch off half the engine to save gas, showed great promise and was considered to be a step ahead of the iconic Packard. Enger shipped his cars nationwide and sent twenty-three all the way to Australia.

The $4 million in capital (more than $100 million today) was to pay for a new plant across the street from Enger's factory in today's Lower Price Hill. The goal was to double the Enger Motor's output. Enger had turned fifty-four, and mid-fall 1916 press reports were bullish on his company. One newspaper reported that it had the capacity to produce 5,000 cars a year at a profit of $1 million.

That $1 million equates to more than $20 million in today's currency, enough for anyone to be enticed into retirement. America's rising auto industry seemed to be Enger's ticket to riches. And it was—but not for long.

The car-making industry was becoming crowded at about the time Enger started dreaming big. Henry Ford set up an assembly plant for his affordable and reliable Model T in downtown Cincinnati in 1915. Ford's Tin Lizzies cost one-third as much as Enger's autos.

The competition across Gest Street from Enger Motor Car Co., former carriage maker Haberer Co., had a huge new factory and was producing a car, the Cino, in multiple models that could compete with Enger cars in quality and performance. The companies' cars received positive press in accounts of distance driving races popular in the early automotive days.

There was more than business pressure on Frank Enger. Social tension was growing in Cincinnati, as anti-German hysteria swelled, fueled by World War I and Germany Emperor Kaiser Wilhelm's refusal to cease sinking non-military ships such as the *Lusitania*. Cincinnatians of German descent like Enger sensed increasing pressure. President Woodrow Wilson, in fact, was just months from asking Congress to declare war on Germany.

Back in their grand mansion in North Avondale, Enger's wife had become seriously ill. With his business and private lives in turmoil, Enger's twelve-cylinder engine could have used a few more spark plugs to ignite his spirits.

It got worse. Unsubstantiated reports circulated that Enger had cancer. Whether the cancer was considered terminal was not reported in Enger's *Cincinnati Enquirer* obituary, but the details of his January 4, 1917, death were.

About 4 p.m. that Thursday, a despondent Enger, who had battled paralysis since he was a boy, was in his office overlooking the downtown skyline. His only living son, John, was on holiday break from Yale University and hanging out with his dad. Franklin told John he expected a phone call in an adjoining room and asked the young man to go there and answer the ring. Shortly after John left his father's office, Frank Enger, who was seated on a couch, placed a gun to his head and pulled the trigger.

According to a news article: "The son hurried to the outer office, and finding there had been no telephone call, returned and found his father stretched on a couch. Blood was flowing from a wound above the father's right ear, and he died within a few minutes without regaining consciousness."

Enger was buried at Spring Grove Cemetery two days later. A subsequent newspaper article quoted an Enger employee as saying his boss' fatal act was caused by "worries of business and physical disability."

Enger left a detailed note to his family describing the cutbacks they needed to make to keep Enger Motor Car Co. running and profitable, but the task was overwhelming. His widow, Pearl Klosterman Enger, had the company placed in receivership that very year, and the courts settled the estate, ultimately valued at more than $7.5 million in today's money.

Pearl Enger and her three children lost their stately Beaux Arts home in the settlement. When built in 1898, it included cutting-edge technology such as an elevator to a grand ballroom on the third floor as well as a bowling alley in the basement.

The elaborate parties held at the family home, known as Enger Hall (now a restored private residence called Marion Hall for its days as a Xavier University residence hall), ceased upon Enger's death. Pearl sold the mansion in 1919 and moved into her son's apartment, where she died of kidney failure on New Year's Day, 1927, at age fifty-six. She was buried next to her husband.

Frank Enger had dreamed of competing against the big boys in the luxury automobile market. Had he lived, perhaps he would have succeeded in keeping Cincinnati on the American auto industry map that Detroit went on to dominate.

He had purchased land and planned to expand his Gest Street domain to Berlin Street, one block east of the old factory, between the Cincinnati-Hamilton-Dayton Railroad tracks and Summer Street. Reacting to German hysteria, however, city officials changed Berlin Street to Woodrow Street about the time Enger learned he was ill.

The five-story, brick Enger factory, though boarded up and showing few clues as to its roots, still stands at Gest and Summer streets. Only one of the Haberer buildings, a warehouse at Gest and Evans streets, survived the 1912 flood. Since the demise of Crosley Motors in 1952, little else is left of Cincinnati's auto industry but the rarely seen historic vehicles it produced.

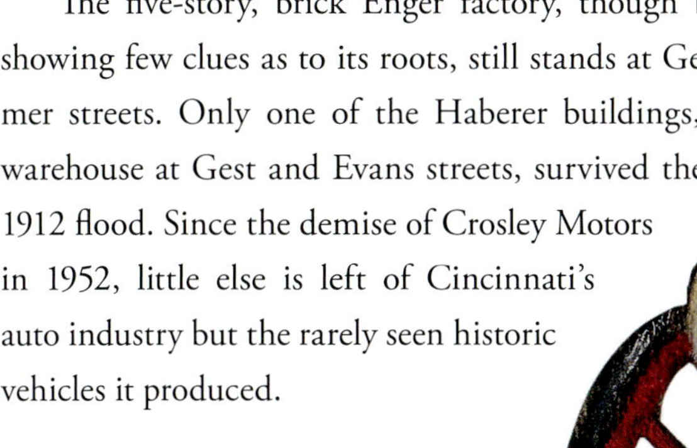

JENNIE PORTER

School principal stuck to her principles

The forty-year career of Jennie Davis Porter—the first African-American woman to earn a doctorate from the University of Cincinnati and to become a school principal in the Queen City—was rocky. To some whose children she sought to educate more than one hundred years ago, and, likely to many parents today, she was a segregationist. To them, her advocacy of Black-only schools was regressive.

Porter felt she was in the right to follow the "racial uplift" leadership of her friend, Booker T. Washington. Both believed that African-American children should be sheltered from society's racial prejudices and that integration should be achieved gradually.

That didn't mean Porter was a segregationist, according to Cincinnati historian Daniel Hurley. Hurley preferred the term "accommodationist." He said Porter lived and advocated the motto on a sign she kept in her office: "Take what you have, and make what you want."

To that end, Porter, who taught art and music at the all-Black Frederick Douglass School in her early career, believed African-American children should not focus entirely on competing with whites for "white-collar" jobs. She believed they should strive for positions they could get and keep, such as trade and domestic work. She also believed she could create more jobs for Black teachers.

This philosophy today would be hotly criticized. Porter's early twentieth century critics, many of whom were aligned with the progressive policies of NAACP leader W.E.B Dubois, were critical, too.

Hurley, however, said understanding the state of education in the late 1880s puts Porter's position in better perspective. An 1887 state law to integrate Cincinnati schools hurt the city's firmly established, all-Black and separate school system. Black teachers lost their jobs, and student enrollment declined. By 1912, city schools had only seven Black teachers and fewer than 300 Black students.

Porter found a way to "accommodate" the situation and give African Americans an alternative. With the financial support of Annie Laws, who was white, Porter established a private kindergarten in the West End for more than one hundred Black students. From that sprung her proposal that Cincinnati Public Schools create the all-Black Harriet Beecher Stowe Elementary School.

Cincinnati Public Schools superintendent Randall Condon and board president John Withrow backed Porter's plan for Stowe School, and the school board accepted it. Classes started there in 1914. A school named for a white abolitionist and run by a Black principal with accredited Black teachers and an all-Black student body was off and running.

But critics such as Wendell Dabney, the NAACP's first local president and forty-six-year editor of the *Union* newspaper, opposed Porter. Dabney called her "Jubilee Jenny" for what he perceived to be Porter's willingness to accept society's racial inequities with a smile. Dabney advocated the NAACP's position that segregated schools hindered young African Americans and set their race back. Integrated schools were the future, Dabney said.

Ultimately, society sided with Dabney. Principal Porter, however, built a successful school and guided many famous students. Some achieved firsts like her. DeHart Hubbard, for example, became the first Black athlete to win an individual Olympic gold medal, soaring to victory in the long jump at the Paris games in 1924.

That same year, former Stowe student Theodore Berry graduated as the valedictorian of integrated Woodward High School. He went on to become a lawyer and the first African American to be elected mayor of Cincinnati (1972–76). Berry also served as president of the local NAACP (1932–46), putting him in the corner opposite his former principal. But the two worked out a compromise, according to Hurley, and co-existed peacefully.

The politically skilled Porter eventually joined the NAACP as a board member, according to her obituary in the *Cincinnati Post*. In addition, she was a trustee at the country's first privately owned historically Black university, Wilberforce, near Xenia, Ohio.

Jennie Davis Porter was born in 1876 to freed Tennessee slave William A. Porter and Edlinda Davis Porter. She was one of the first African-American teachers in Cincinnati, and he was Cincinnati's first Black undertaker. According to an article published by the Cincinnati History Library and Archives, Porter attended integrated public schools. She graduated from Hughes High School and started teaching three years later, opening the first all-Black kindergarten with women's rights advocate Annie Laws.

Porter ran Stowe School, starting in 1914 and attended UC at night, beginning in 1918 when she was forty-two. As one of a small number of African-American students at UC, she fought off prejudice and earned three degrees: a bachelor's in 1923, a master's in 1925 and a doctorate in 1928.

She published articles on African-American education and social issues in national magazines throughout her career and, according to her 1936 obituary in the *Cincinnati Times-Star*, she was "active in every move, national and local, to advance her race for the last twenty-five years" of her life.

Stowe School, which Porter called "the greatest interest in my life," had been a hit from the beginning, growing from an initial enrollment of 350 to 1,300 in 1922. It offered traditional academics and vocational and agricultural programs.

To provide her students with inspiration, Porter hosted prominent African-American role models and rights activists at Stowe. They included scientist George Washington Carver, singer Marian Anderson, singer/actor Paul Robeson and writer Langston Hughes.

Porter directed Stowe School until heart illness forced her to take a leave of absence in 1935. She died the next year at fifty-nine in her Walnut Hills home. The Stowe School closed in 1962. The school board named a now-gone junior high school after Porter in 1953, and today, Hays-Porter Elementary in the West End neighborhood, offers its students a high technology education.

Porter's grave and those of many abolitionists and members of the Underground Railroad are in the historically Black Union Baptist Cemetery on Cleves-Warsaw Pike in West Price Hill.